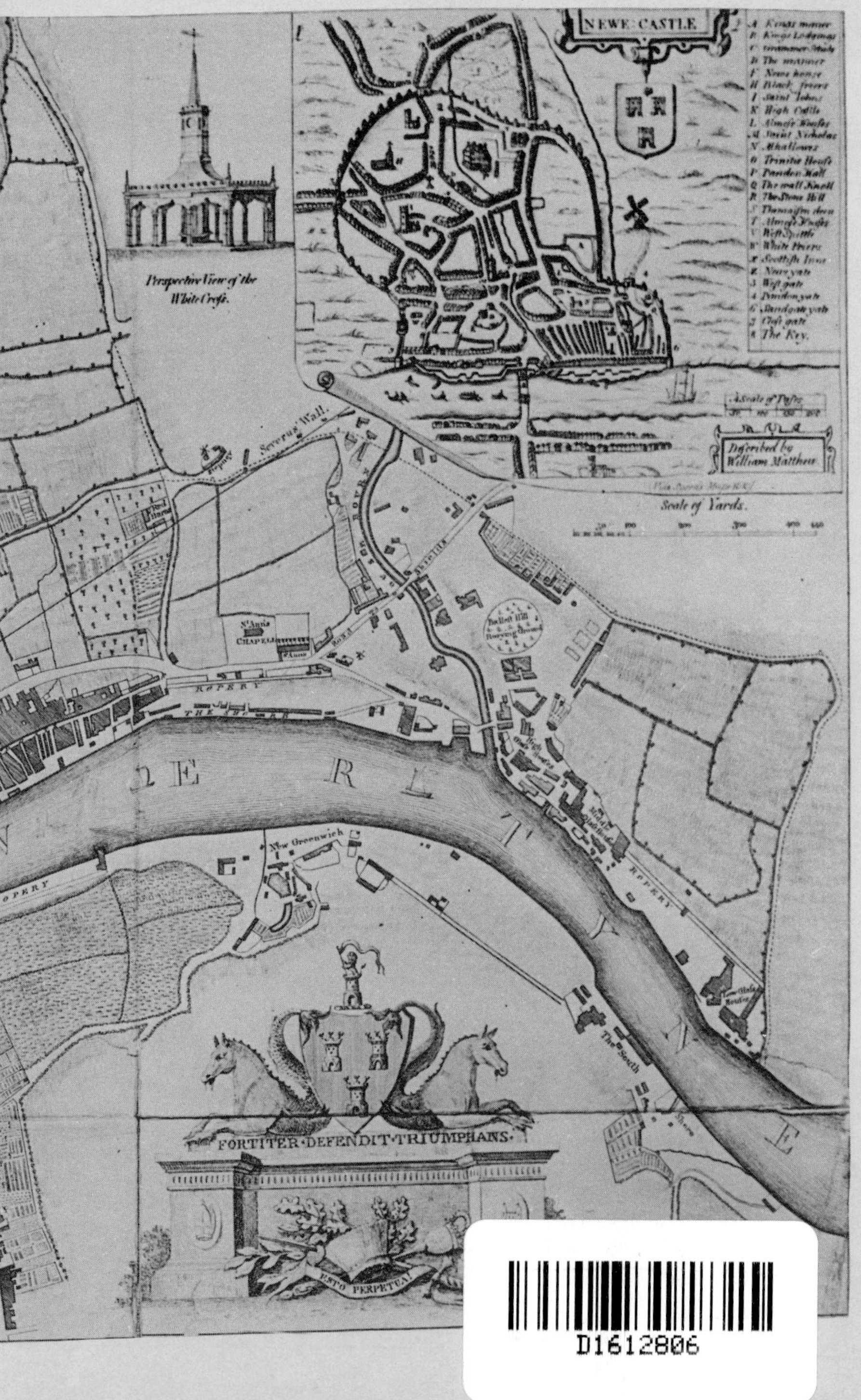

NEWE CASTLE
D The manner
H Black freers
K High Castle
M Saint Nicholas
N Alhallows
O Trinitie House
P Pandon Hall
Q The wall Knoll
R The Stone Hill
W White Freers
3 West gate
4 Pandon yate
6 Sandgate yate
8 The Key.
A Scale of Paces
Described by William Matthew
Perspective View of the White Cross.
Severus Wall.
Scale of Yards.
S.t Ann's CHAPELL
ROPERY
New Greenwich
Ballast Hill
FORTITER·DEFENDIT·TRIUMPHANS·
ESTO PERPETUA!

EIGHTEENTH-CENTURY NEWCASTLE

EIGHTEENTH-CENTURY NEWCASTLE

by

P. M. Horsley

ORIEL PRESS

First Published 1971
ISBN 0 85362 091 1
Library of Congress Catalog Card No. 79-112720

Published by
Oriel Press Limited.
32 Ridley Place,
Newcastle upon Tyne,
England. NE1 8LH.
Printed in 11/13pt Baskerville.
Printed by J. & P. Bealls Ltd., Newcastle.

ACKNOWLEDGEMENTS

THIS IS the first time these essays have been published in book form. Several have already appeared in *Parsons Journal* and I wish to express my sincere gratitude to C. A. Parsons and Company Limited for permission to reprint them.

I am glad to have the opportunity of acknowledging also the courteous help and interest of:
The City Archivist; the Freemen; the Director and Curator of the Laing Art Gallery; the Librarian and staff of the Central Reference Library, Jesmond Branch Library, the Literary and Philosophical Society, the Society of Antiquaries, the University Library; the Keeper of the University Museum of Antiquaries; Captain E. Cottew Brown, Secretary of Trinity House; Mr. J. Davidson, Secretary of Reid and Sons, Limited; Mr. W. A. Fawcett, Secretary of Newcastle Stock Exchange; Mr. T. V. Roberts, House Governor and Secretary and Mr. C. F. Naylor, Hospital Secretary of the United Newcastle upon Tyne Hospitals; Mr. A. Walker, Secretary of the Mining Institute; Mr. L. Wallace, lately of the Royal French Arms; Mr. K. R. Whitehall, Managing Director, Raine and Company Limited; Dr. H. A. Wilson, all of Newcastle upon Tyne: the County Archivist; the Borough Librarian, Blyth; Mr. F. Hetherington, Estate Office, Seaton Delaval Hall; Mr. W. Hugonin, Estates Office, Alnwick, all of Northumberland: the Department of Palaeontology and Diplomatic, University of Durham: Mr. G. N. Drinkwater, lately of the Shipley Art Gallery and Mr. E. H. Kirkup, lately of Strathmore Estate Offices, Gateshead upon Tyne: the

Director of the Central Library, Sunderland: the Proprietors of the *Glasgow Herald* and the Director of Museums and Art Galleries, Glasgow: the librarian and staff of the Sandeman Public Library, Perth: Mr. R. G. E. Jarvis, Doddington Hall, Lincs: Henry Spencer and Sons, Retford: Mr. E. A. Carson, H.M. Customs and Excise, King's Beam House; the Librarian and staff of the Courtauld Institute of Art and of the Royal Academy of Arts; Mr. R. E. C. Lander, Shipping Editor of Lloyd's; the Departmental Record Officer, Post Office Records; Mr. D. S. Lavender; Christie, Mansion and Woods, Limited; Phillips, Son and Neale; Sotheby and Company; Miss A. Stanley, Literary Department, Somerset House; Sir Anthony Wagner, K.C.V.O., F.S.A., Garter King of Arms, all of London: Monsieur Le Conservateur, Bibliothèque Nationale, and Monsieur le Chef de Service, Louvre, Paris: the Librarian and staff of the Frick Art Reference Library and of the Newhouse Galleries, New York; the Chief Curator of the National Gallery of Art, Washington, D.C.

Newcastle upon Tyne P. M. Horsley
1970

CONTENTS

The Great Bridge of Tyne after the Flood (1771)

I

TYNE BRIDGE

Saturday, 16 *November* 1771; 10 *p.m.*

Trade had been poor. Incessant rain, accompanied by a north-easter, had kept the usual crowds away. Disgruntled shop-keepers had put up their shutters and gone early to bed with the familiar sound of the Tyne washing against the sterlings and an occasional creak from the old wooden houses. The water was running fast but no one was over-anxious. The cellar doors, opening onto the river, were safely bolted; all the stock, glass and leather, cheese, books and hardware, haberdashery and millinery, shoes, gloves, flax and bales of cloth were under cover. Much of the property belonged to the Corporation who made no difficulty about the renewal of leases. The Ashworths and Atkinsons, John Grey and George Weatherley had security of tenure for another twenty years. They could enjoy untroubled sleep. Only the Oliphants at the Gateshead end were restless but they had not spent a peaceful night since they were charged with murder. Although they were acquitted, their neighbours had cold-shouldered them for seven long years and the doctor's once flourishing practice had dwindled away.

Saturday, 16 *November* 1771; 11 *p.m.*

The rain continued. At 11 o'clock Solway Moss lifted, surged over rich farmlands and released the flood-waters in the north-west. To the east the feeders of South Tyne swelled the raging torrents; the river, soon to reach a level unparalleled in living memory, began a headlong descent down valley, sweeping all before it—buildings, crops, cattle and people. Far away in Newcastle the current swirled and sucked at the foundations of the old bridge, which stirred uneasily in the rain-swept night.

It was indeed an old bridge, wise in the ways of nature and of men. Opened in 1250, two years after its wooden predecessor and Newcastle town had been destroyed by a mysterious fire—God's avenging flame, according to the thirteenth-century chronicler, Matthew Prior—the bridge had ever since formed a narrow but busy section of the King's Highway to Scotland and its graceful silhouette won nation-wide acclaim.

In conformity with medieval building techniques the piers rested on sterlings, themselves supported by stilts driven into the river-bed. These foundations were never modernised and were liable to damage by sudden floods, drift ice and, as Newcastle's coal trade expanded, the impact of heavily-laden keels, thrown off-course by the currents. The free water between the piers, already restricted by the sterlings, suffered further contraction from the silt, aggravated by four centuries of ballast-dumping. In 1765 it was calculated that 100,000 tons, chiefly gravel and sand, were being carried annually to the Tyne and transferred by keels and lighters to be piled up into ballast heaps, one of which flanked the Ouseburn. Some of the ballast fell into the river accidentally; keelmen were accused of shovelling it overboard through laziness; high winds blew it into mid-stream[1] where the tides washed it over the river-bed. Officialdom loudly bewailed the growing evil but could not, or would not, find the money to implement various practical suggestions such as Liddle's scheme (1755) for carrying ballast out to sea in hoppers.[2]

To support the roadway the bridge had twelve low stone arches, some of which were eventually closed by quays and warehouses. The width between the parapets was 15 feet, reduced in several places to 9 feet by houses, shops, gates and the chapel of St. Thomas the Martyr. As road transport developed, an ever-increasing number of unwieldy carts rumbled across, destroying the surface and putting a greater

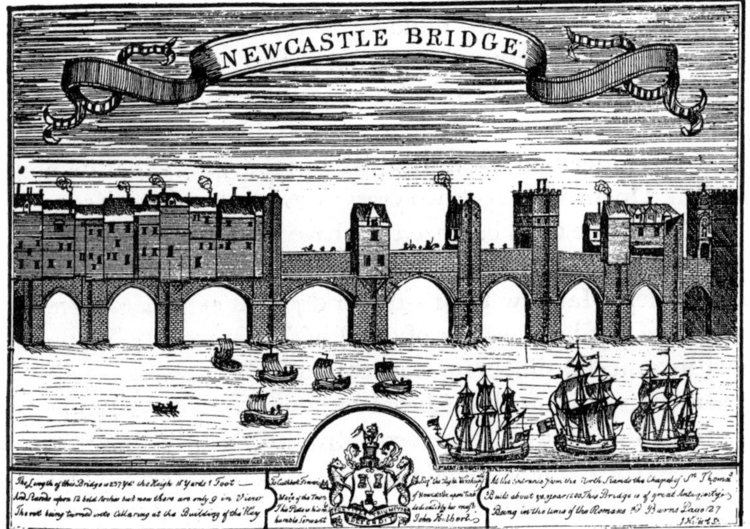

Old Tyne Bridge

strain on the arches than they were ever intended to bear. From time to time the structure was repaired but the work was as haphazard as the methods used for raising the necessary funds.

Until 1417 a keeper, originally the priest in charge of the chapel, but later a layman appointed by the Common Council, was responsible for the collection and allocation of money for the maintenance of the whole bridge. In that year the Court of Chancery confirmed the long and bitterly contested claim of the Bishops of Durham to the ownership of one third at the southern end.[3] This decision was received with an ill-grace by Newcastle, who never lost an opportunity of reviving the dispute, although they were now relieved of the preservation of 180 feet of masonry and timber and were desperately short of money for the upkeep of the rest.

What they had, came from sources which sound strange to modern ears. In the thirteenth century the Archbishop of York, the Bishops of Durham, Rochester, Caithness and Waterford offered indulgences of ten to thirty days to anyone who would provide cash or labour for the reparation of Tyne Bridge. Legacies were left by the faithful for the support

Tower on the Old Bridge 1763

of the bridge and prayers for the repose of the donors' souls. Equally pious gifts of land or property provided rents from parts of Jesmond, Sandyford, Pandon and Byker and from houses inside the walls. Of the latter the best-paying was the famous 'Earl's Inn of Northumberland' which brought in 20s. a year. Unfortunately, tenants were apt to default and in the fourteenth century when repairs were urgently needed, the town's magistrates ordered a levy of arrears together with a ten-years' imposition of pontage on all goods unloaded at Newcastle quay. Various Guilds—the Fullers and Dyers, Glaziers, Goldsmiths, Weavers and Cordwainers—added their quota. Half the fines incurred for using abusive language to fellow-members and for the heinous crime of accepting a Scotsman as apprentice or journeyman were ear-marked for the bridge. Occasionally a crown grant was forthcoming. Richard III allotted £40 annually 'during pleasure' and

John Smeaton
By courtesy of the Director, The Science Museum, London

Henry VIII £20. Both grants lapsed with disconcerting suddenness so in 1577 the mayor, with commendable astuteness, petitioned for the renewal of the former. In the days of Charles I the royal finances were in as parlous a state as those of the bridge. However, in 1649, in gratitude perhaps for the consideration he had received as a prisoner in Newcastle, he permitted several of the royal trees in Chopwell Woods to be used for maintenance work.

The last repairs carried out on Tyne Bridge were financed by Bishop Trevor. In 1769 he engaged Smeaton to report on the state of his section. Smeaton advised him that although the bridge was originally ill-built and in a general state of disrepair, it might 'by occasional repairs, seasonably applied, last many year.' His estimate of £150–£200 for what he termed a 'kind of jobbing work' was accepted, the work put in hand and the bridge reopened to traffic on 19 July 1770.

Sunday, 17 *November* 1771; 2 *a.m.*

The sound of the rain was lost in the roar of flood-water, now perilously close to the keystones of the arches.

It is said that before the waters close finally over his head, a drowning man sees his whole life in retrospect. Tyne Bridge, silent spectator of five centuries of human life, its triumphs and disasters, laughter and tears, cruelty and kindness, was drowning.

The most spectacular scene Tyne Bridge had ever witnessed was the vast concourse assembled in July 1503, to greet the child-bride Margaret, daughter of Henry VII, on her way to marry James IV of Scotland. John Young, Somerset Herald, has left an eye-witness account of the glittering procession, headed by the Prior of Tynemouth and the Earl of Northumberland with their retinues, which made its way down the steep Bottle Bank onto the bridge. There the young princess was received by representatives of the religious orders, their crosses gleaming in the sun, by the mayor, sheriffs and aldermen, all 'well apoynted' and by surpliced choirs of children. Through gaily decorated streets, crowded with well-wishers 'in so grett nombre that it was a playsur for to se', she passed to her lodging in the Austin Friary. No evil portent marred the rejoicings.

Ten years later her return journey went unnoticed, the return of the widow whose husband lay dead on Flodden Field.

Just before sunset a more modest procession used to leave Sheriff Hill, where the circuit judges were met by the High Sheriff of Northumberland and escorted to Newcastle for the opening of the assizes. The splendour depended, not upon the reputation of the judges, but upon the popularity or otherwise of the sheriff. The gathering shadows of night were surely symbolic of the fate of many a sorry wretch awaiting trial. In 1528 householders on the bridge saw the heads and quarters of a band of Border thieves displayed on the keep of the castle. Their grandchildren watched one day while Sandrs Cheisman's workman built a pinnacle on the bridge and a labourer came along to hang on it the head of William Waterson, cruelly put to death because he was a seminary priest.

One of the aldermen who had welcomed Princess Margaret was George Bird, tenant of the 'Earl's Inn' in the Close, who decided to improve the view of the bridge from his windows by the erection of a tower on the third pier. Until 1771 this tower was used as a prison for petty offenders. One of the last inmates was a luckless pitman's wife caught stealing a loin of mutton from a stall in the Flesh Market three days before Christmas.

Even less welcome arrivals than the judges were the Scots. They came in 1640. The rout of Charles I's army at Newburn opened the way to royalist Newcastle. On 30 August the mayor and those dignitaries who, in the words of Lieutenant-colonel Sir John Fenwick, 'were not so nimble at flight as Sir John Marley', humbly awaited on the bridge the appearance of General Leslie who led the victorious Convenanters into a half-empty town, its shops shuttered and trade at a standstill. In 1644 the Scots came again. On this occasion Sir John Marley, now mayor, inspired the townsmen to a gallant, though unavailing stand. From the bridge could be seen the thin line of defenders manning the walls, their outlines hazy in the flames and smoke from Sandgate which had been fired to delay the Scottish advance. The bridge itself was in the hands of the Earl of Callender who was joined by General Leven for the investment of the town. For ten bitter weeks fifteen hundred men withstood the assault of thirty thousand. Then the keep of the castle, last resort of the defiant mayor, fell to the enemy. The dazed survivors were left to bury their dead, tend their wounded and repair their battered houses.

They had their revenge. For the third time in a decade the Scots marched to Newcastle. In 1650 after Leslie's crushing defeat by Cromwell at Dunbar, the heart-sick prisoners were 'driven like Turkeys to Newcastle in England, where about 1,600 of them were starv'd, having nothing to eat but green cabbage leaves, and Oats in a small Proportion'.[4] They were lodged overnight in St. Nicholas' Church where twenty-three died of exhaustion. The survivors shambled over Tyne Bridge on their way to Durham and eventual deportation to the sugar plantations of the West Indies. Newcastle Common Council books record an expenditure of £6 for providing candles and coals for the guards, cleaning the church and paying All Saints' sexton fourpence per grave.

It was not only invaders who caused havoc in the town. Tyne Bridge could recall not a few riots. There was once a pretty lovers' lane near the Ballast Hills, much frequented on Sundays by apprentices and their lasses. During the week the area provided an excellent drying-ground for household washing. On this popular spot one Christopher Reasley dared to build a lime-kiln. In 1633 protesting apprentices celebrated their Shrove Tuesday holiday by wrecking the kiln, attacking Reasley's house with pikes and halberds, barring the Sandgate against the forces of law and order and defying arrest. The authorities appealed in vain for the support of the townsfolk who nursed other grievances against the corporation. They were indeed busy enumerating their complaints in a petition to the King, which proved as ineffectual as the apprentices' demonstration.

Some fifty years later, when Newcastle declared for the Prince of Orange, a hot-headed mob rushed to the Sandhill where there stood an equestrian statue[5] of James II cast in brass. Amid jeers and yells the statue was manhandled down to the quay below the bridge and into the river it went with a mighty splash. Tradition suggests that this senseless act was abetted by Colonel Heyford, commander of the garrison, whose troops, armed with swords and carbines, stood by to prevent any interference by the civil authorities. But the statue was yet to play its part in Newcastle life. Afterwards it was salvaged and the Common Council of 1695 allocated one leg of the horse to St. Andrew's Church and the rest of the animal to All Saints' to provide new bells.[6] All Saints' bells were cast in a foundry in Manor Chare, possibly by men who tumbled the statue into the river, over which their peal rang out for a hundred years.

Equestrian Statue of James II

The Corn riots of 1740 were a more serious affair. The first rumblings of discontent among pitmen, keelmen and the poor of the town were silenced by the raising of the militia and an official promise that the price of corn would be reduced.[7]

A fortnight passed during which the corporation, with considerable lack of foresight, disbanded the militia. Not only was the price of corn unchanged: the shops and warehouses were closed and there was none to be bought. Then the mayor convened a meeting of leading townsmen to discuss the situation. The venue was the Guildhall on the Sandhill which was rapidly surrounded by a blustering mob, bent on mischief. The unlucky committee member detailed to report progress to the crowd was knocked down and trampled underfoot by a seething mass who stormed the Guildhall, attacked the committee and ransacked the rooms, destroying the public

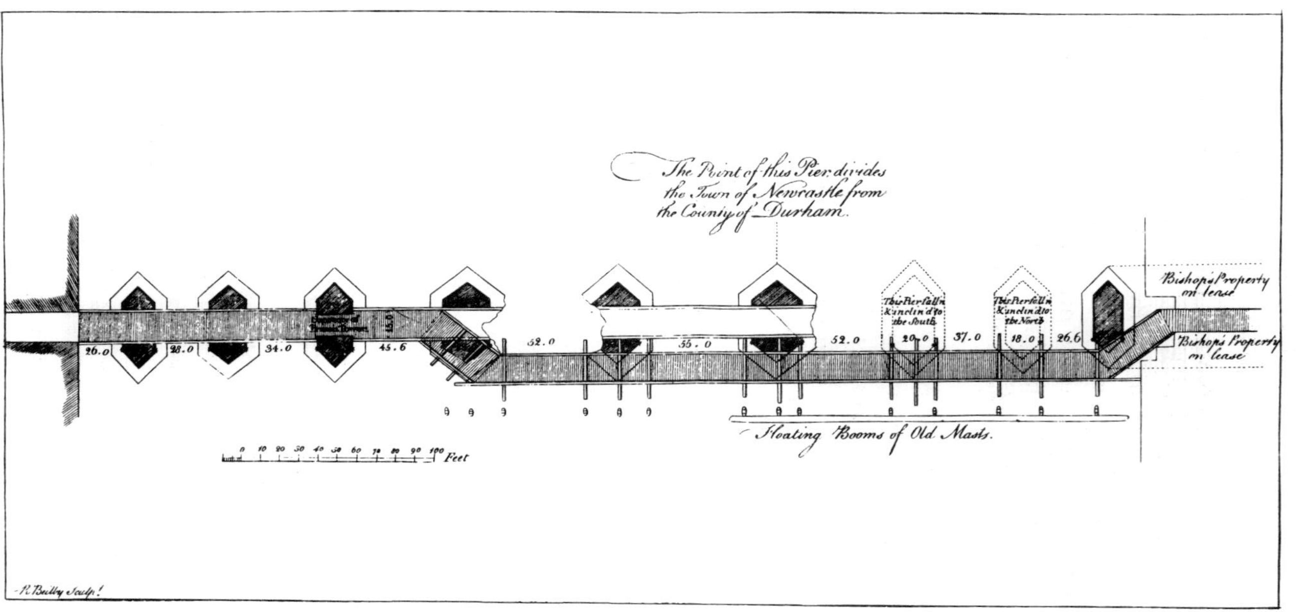

Plan of the ruined bridge by Ralph Beilby

records and making off with whatever they could carry away. All that day the rioters roamed the streets and the quayside, where a grain-ship was lying, terrorising passers-by and threatening to burn the town. By evening three companies of Howard's regiment arrived from Alnwick and dispersed the trouble-makers, taking forty prisoners. The next time the judges rode in from Sheriff Hill they convicted six, and another dejected little group trudged over Tyne Bridge on the way to transportation.

On the bridge itself was a town in miniature, whose inhabitants had an uninterrupted view of the life ashore which was reflected in their restricted confines; births and deaths, work and play, heavy traffic when trade was good, an uncanny silence during depressions, tragedy and comedy.

Tyne Bridge laughed with the people when two he-asses staged a battle royal on the narrow roadway. Even the buxom country-woman who was bitten as she tried to pass the combatants went home 'in tolerable spirits,'[8] after treatment at the Infirmary. The bridge could identify the six ruffians who set about a newsvendor one dark night and inflicted serious injuries on their victim.[9] Only the bridge saw Dr. Oliphant's maid jump from the cellar door at low tide, pick herself up from the sand and run towards Bottle Bank, but not even the bridge knew how her strangled body got into the Tyne at Dunston.

Sunday 17 *November* 1771; 3.30 *a.m.*

The brief interval for retrospect was over. 'God had sent a warning to a sinful people.'[10] The bridge shuddered at the ruthless pressure of the floodwater which the weakened piers and arches could no longer withstand.

Weatherley the shoemaker awoke. Peering into the night he could barely distinguish his neighbour Fiddas guiding his wife, children and maid along the roadway, now awash. Hastily collecting his own family, Weatherley turned north. The next-door house crashed into the river. He turned south, only to face a huge gap. Two arches had fallen. Terror-stricken, numb with exposure, the family huddled for six interminable hours on a small slab until they were rescued by a heroic Gateshead bricklayer named Woodward. Weatherley had lost his home, shop and stock but he was safe. He could build up a new life. Not so his neighbour who, against his better judgement, went back with the maid to retrieve her belongings. A distraught Mrs. Fiddas, standing at the bridge-end, saw an arch collapse and carry with it her husband and the girl. Byerley the ironmonger and his son, Ann Tinkler the draper, the apprentice of James the cheesemonger, were all drowned that morning and two bridge-dwellers died later from shock. Byerley's body was found in the ruins six months later; Ann Tinkler's was not recovered until the following July.

Booksellers, flax-dealers, milliners, glovers watched helplessly as their livelihood was swept away.[11] Many owed their lives to the unflagging efforts of their parish priest, Andrew Wood, Rector of Gateshead. Among those saved were the Oliphants who found temporary shelter in Church Chare[12] but this last adversity drove them to seek seclusion in the doctor's native Scotland.

Sunday 17 *November* 1771; 10 *a.m.*

Daylight revealed the magnitude of the catastrophe. The river was running eight feet above the high-water mark of an average spring tide. Thomas Bewick the engraver, helping in the rescue work, rowed about the Sandhill flooded to a depth of six feet. Low-lying property was submerged; ships had been lifted onto the quay; timber and merchandise together with the customs shed, washed off. From Newcastle to Shields both banks of the Tyne were littered with stranded keels and debris. Jarrow Slake took much of the flood-water, thus saving North and South Shields from inundation. There, by a strange quirk of fate, floated the house of Patten the draper of Tyne Bridge. In it, unharmed were the family pets, a cat and a dog. By four o'clock that afternoon the flood-waters had subsided.

The time had come for the appraisal of the damage and the organization of resources. There were many to help and regrettably, many to hinder.

Local cartmen promptly raised the price of coal by 3s. a load but their bid for easy money was foiled by the coal-owners who equally promptly refused to supply would-be profiteers. Looters presented a graver problem. A lone horseman riding one night by Jarrow Slake saw a wagon laden with timber and pulled by three horses; he failed to intercept it. He reported his encounter to the Whitburn justices who offered a reward for information leading to a conviction. The gentlemen of South Shields banded together and, with a detachment of troops from Tynemouth, cleared the district of plunderers. Newcastle Common Council ordered all persons salvaging timber from Sparrowhawk to Hedwin Stream to report their finds to the water-bailiff. The promise of a reasonable reward or the institution of proceedings of the utmost severity indicated the appropriate line of conduct to pursue.

On 18 December an official subscription list for the relief of the flood victims was opened by the Mayor, Sir Walter Blackett. By the end of the following March over £4,000 had been raised for distribution in Newcastle and Gateshead. Local churchmen, titled families, the Corporation, unnamed individuals from Scotland to Cambridge contributed to these funds. A house-to-house collection in Gateshead amounted to £400. The last subscription recorded in the local press was one of £20, sent by the London Free Masons for the benefit of three members of St. Nicholas' Lodge who had lived and worked on Tyne Bridge.

The fall of the bridge severed road communications between north and south. Interim measures were hastily adopted.

His Majesty's mail was rowed across the Tyne by day and by night and within ten days of the disaster, a free ferry 'commodious and safe', plied during daylight hours between the Swirle in Sandgate and the south bank.[13] It did not long remain free. On 6 January 1772, a lengthy and complicated scale of charges for every conceivable combination of freight, human, animal and material, was enforced until further notice by Thomas Valentine and Robert Sadler—appointed collectors by the Tyne Bridge and Ferry Committee. According to James Murray[14] the ferry was far from commodious and one of the collectors whom, with uncharacteristic discretion, he does not name, a petty tyrant.

> You must wait the pleasure of a little arbitrary bashaw, who will not move one foot beyond the rules of his authority—Four rowers in a small boat drag the ponderous ferry across the river very slowly. From the time we entered the boat, before we landed on the opposite side, an hour was almost spent.

The visiting judges took one look at these arrangements and opted for the mayoral barge.

At the beginning of December demolition work began on the old bridge in preparation for the erection of a temporary structure, the first pile of which was not driven until the following July. The intervening months were largely spent in a revival of the long-standing conflict with the Bishop of Durham and in obtaining the assent of Parliament. John Egerton had taken up his appointment only three months before the disastrous floods. As yet unaware of the bitterness of this local rivalry, he was nevertheless an astute business

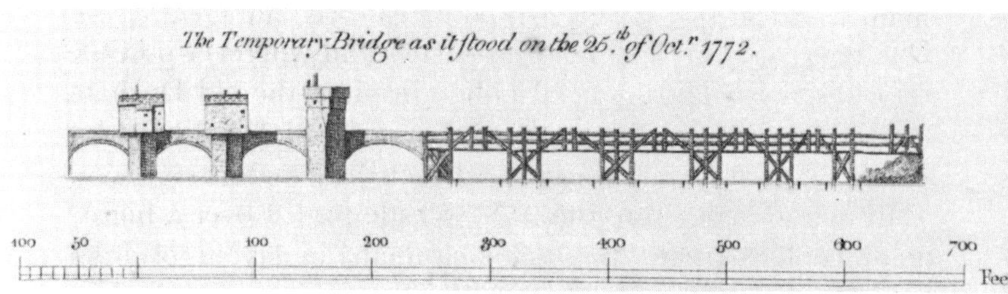

The Temporary Bridge 1772

John Egerton, Bishop of Durham

man. It is said that on his arrival he engaged an agent called Due to reassess his leasehold properties and wherever possible raise the rents. His financial policy inspired the old Durham toast: 'May the Lord take the Bishop and the Devil have his Due.' Newcastle Corporation had met their match.

In appointing a consultant Newcastle passed over a highly qualified local man, William Chapman, in favour of John Smeaton with John Wooler of Whitby as his junior. Robert Mylne was engaged by the burgesses of Gateshead, on the advice of their Rector. This loved and respected priest was not to see the outcome of his exertions. His health, impaired

Robert Mylne, Architect

by his rescue work during the flood, deteriorated under the continued strain. On 15 March 1772 he was buried in the choir of his own church, where the people of Gateshead erected a tablet to his memory, in token of their esteem, affection and gratitude.

Before the experts published their reports, two far-sighted proposals appeared in the local press. The first advocated a high level bridge from the top of Bottle Bank to the head of Dean Street; the second was the workmanlike plan of Hutchinson, a master-mason, for a high level bridge from the Javel Group to Pipewellgate, the site eventually chosen in the mid-nineteenth century. He listed the advantages of such a bridge —easier and more attractive approaches, a freer flow of increasingly heavy traffic, space for a 300 foot extension of the quay, all of which could be obtained with the minimum demolition of existing property and no interference with conditions in the lower parts of the town. 'As we build for posterity,' he wrote, 'let us do it in such a manner that remotest ages may approve the justice and dignity of the plan.'

Newcastle Corporation was clearly interested in this site but they were waiting for Smeaton's report which they received in January 1772. In his view the old Tyne Bridge, too narrow and too low, difficult of approach from Bottle Bank with its dangerous gradient of 1 in 7 to 8, was a total loss. To restore the gaps in the bridge without the use of sterlings would be extremely difficult and he could not give an accurate estimate of either the time required or the cost of such an undertaking. A reproduction of the old bridge on the same site would take at least three and a half years to complete at a cost of £25,000 and would have all the disadvantages of its predecessor. Temporary repairs to the remains of the old structure would involve an expenditure of about £2,400 and render it serviceable for seven years, during which time a new bridge could be built on a different site.

Smeaton suggested a low level bridge from the Javel Group, with seven higher arches. The width between the parapets would be at least 30 feet; there would be a pedestrian way on each side but no buildings whatsoever. The northern end would open onto the Close, the southern onto Pipewellgate. An approach road would run from Bottle Bank via what is now Half-Moon Lane, the minimum width of which would be 40 feet, and the gradient reduced to 1 in 19 to 20. Such a bridge would cost £50,000, exclusive of road works and property purchases. The latter would certainly be opposed and in any event be a heavy item, but Smeaton held that the claims of public convenience far outweighed those of private ownership.

Opposition was soon forthcoming, for Bottle Bank, the Via Regia of ancient documents, was not only the royal but indeed the only road leading through Gateshead to Tyne Bridge.

Apart from repairs on special occasions such as the passage of Charles I on his way to be crowned in Scotland[16], its upkeep had been a constant charge upon the parish. Furthermore, despite the steep gradient and frequent traffic congestion, it was the hub of Gateshead's commerce. Over 60 per cent of the tradesmen had premises there.

The burgesses of Gateshead were naturally indignant and alarmed at the prospect of seeing their main thoroughfare by-passed. By the end of January the entire population had appealed for help to the Rector, Andrew Wood, who wrote to the Lord Bishop, John Egerton, a Londoner by birth, imploring his protection and assistance. In the course of his reasoned arguments Wood explained to this newcomer that Gateshead was to Newcastle what the Borough of Southwark was to the City of London. He followed up this apt analogy with the shrewd reminder that the rents from his Lordship's leasehold estates in the affected areas would diminish if trade declined. For the sake of Gateshead's prosperity the bridge must be rebuilt on the old site or as near it as might be. John Egerton was quick to grasp the situation and lent his unqualified support to the borough.

Newcastle Corporation, who favoured Smeaton's projected Javel Group site, found him adamant. He had no intention of risking heavy losses in revenue, paying out vast sums to property owners or of saddling his successors with a crippling debt. On behalf of the See of Durham he declared himself willing to repair the two piers and three arches on the Gateshead end of the old bridge. If a new bridge was built on the old site, he would require compensation for the losses sustained on his section. If a new site was selected, he disclaimed all liability for removing any part of the old bridge, standing or fallen, or for contributing to the upkeep of a new bridge.

At this juncture Mylne was commissioned to make a report. One feels a certain sympathy for him. Having no wish to offend either his colleagues or the powerful Corporation of Newcastle or the equally powerful Bishop of Durham, he had to tread warily in this supercharged atmosphere.

St. Thomas' Chapel, Bridge End

In his report (12 March 1772) he reviewed with strict impartiality the various interests, rights and obligations involved but made it clear that in his opinion, a new bridge on the old site was the best solution to the problem. He had some misgivings about the existing approaches but he was reasonably certain that property owners on the east side of

Bottle Bank from High Church Chair to the river were 'willing to part with their houses for the accommodation of the public on receiving equivalent satisfaction', thus allowing the construction of a 40-foot wide road with an easier gradient. He advocated a similar road from the Close at the Newcastle end, deprecated any attempt to improve the Side and suggested that traffic should use Butcher Bank which could be widened. It was at this point that Mylne allowed himself one sly dig at the Newcastle authorities.

Were it not for the lenity of the police, which in this instance seems to border on neglect, in allowing encroachments of various nuisances on the breadth of the way (Butcher Bank), there would be, at this time, a tolcrable passageway for carriages.

Newcastle then consulted Wooler who despite his earlier collaboration with Smeaton, advised a new bridge on the old site 'unless the impracticability of that measure be proved and acknowledged.' He added a warning that any party seeking to establish such impracticability would be embarking upon not only a hazardous but a very costly experiment.

The Mayor and Common Council could ill afford to indulge in any such costly ventures. After mortifying deliberations they reluctantly abandoned the Javel Group scheme. The Bishop of Durham had won the day.

In due course Parliament sanctioned the erection of a temporary and a permanent bridge. In the imposing list of trustees appear the names of John Greene, successor to Andrew Wood, William Chapman, hitherto ignored, and William Hilton, poet and bookseller, whose shop on the old bridge had been destroyed by the floods. Mylne estimated two months for the building of the temporary bridge 'if set about with alacrity and spirit'. Newcastle called for an all-out effort to complete it by New Year's Day, 1773.[17] Wooler would not commit himself to a definite date. Finally a four-months' time limit was set. The work was given to John Stephenson[18] who, under the threat of a heavy penalty for non-fulfilment of his contract, displayed the requisite alacrity and spirit. The first

Vaults under St. Thomas' Chapel showing blocking-in of arch

pile was driven on 17 July and the bridge opened for traffic 27 October 1772. Stephenson's workmen celebrated the occasion by marching through the town with banners flying and music at their head. The Common Council was otherwise engaged. Inevitably the original estimate, of which they had guaranteed £2,400, was exceeded. They had therefore, to elect a committee of ways and means to clear the debt incurred. They were to face a far greater deficit in respect of the permanent bridge. By 29 December 1778, the Corporation had spent £21,042, 16s. 11d., which included £1,838, 9s. 8d., the price of the property on their part of the old bridge, and they reckoned that they would have to find an additional £10,000 for the completion of the structure and compensation for property due to be demolished during the widening of the approaches.

Mylne was the engineer for the three arches of the southern section, Wooler for the remainder. In February 1774, handbills and advertisements in the local papers announced vacancies for masons. Interim supplies of dressed stone were already available and quarries were opened at Elswick and St. Anthony's, while the Bishop of Durham obtained his material from the quarry behind Oakwellgate. Mylne got off to a flying start. The Bishop laid his foundation stone on 14 October amid general rejoicing from the burgesses of Gateshead. On 25 April of the following year Sir Matthew White Ridley performed a similar ceremony at Newcastle 'amidst a great concourse of people, who ardently wished prosperity and permanence to the undertaking.'[19]

In 1776 a commemorative copper medal was deposited in the pier marking the boundary between the two towns. The demarcation line was later clearly defined by letting the famous Blue Stone into the pavement. On 13 September 1779, the last Newcastle arch was closed and the workmen again marched in procession through the streets, this time to a feast provided by the Mayor. Traffic began to rumble across the 300 foot-long Town Bridge on 30 April 1781. Designed primarily for utility, it was well-proportioned with buttressed piers, nine rounded arches and an angular recess at every pier. This minor embellishment vanished within twenty years when the increasing volume of traffic demanded a wider roadway.

Unlike its picturesque predecessor, this bridge was not destined to stand as a mute witness of five centuries of history. In the span of a man's lifetime it was rubbing shoulders with

Newcastle upon Tyne from the south showing the new Town Bridge

the High Level Bridge[20] and smoke from the new-fangled locomotives billowed round its arches in a west wind. The development of rail traffic was matched by progress in shipping. Modern steamers could not pass under the low arches of the Town Bridge which fell victim to a mechanical age. It was pulled down in 1866 to make way for the latest engineering triumph, the Swing Bridge, built at a total cost of £233,000 and opened to traffic in 1876.

So you can still cross the Tyne where Oliphants and Byerleys, Weatherleys and Tinklers, Hiltons and Pattens crossed two hundred years ago. The surroundings have changed out of all recognition but you will have one thing in common with them. From the bottom of Bottle Bank to Half-Moon Lane you must negotiate, by car or on foot, a gradient of 1 in 6½.

NOTES

1. In December 1764, 1,000 tons were washed off St. Anthony's Quay in one night.
2. At an enquiry in Newcastle (2 August 1848) by the Harbour Department of the Admiralty, keelmen of thirty and forty years' experience complained of similar conditions and admitted that they were afraid of night trips under the High Level Bridge.
3. The Blue Stone, which marked the boundary, is still to be seen in the Keep of the Castle.
4. Laurence Echard, chaplain to the Archbishop of Canterbury, in his *History of England*, 1720.
5. The work of William Larson, it had been approved by Sir Christopher Wren and cost the town £800.
6 In 1707 the figure of James II was bought by Samuel Smith, a well-known bell-founder of York, who was advised by his uncle to preserve the head and shoulders, very well-wrought and very entire, as a garden ornament.
7. Prices were fixed at: Wheat 7s.; rye 5s.; oats 2s. 6d.; maslin 5s. 6d. per boll.
8. *Newcastle Journal*, 30 June 1764
9. *Newcastle Courant*, 20–23 February 1711/12. Ten shillings reward was offered by the proprietor for information leading to the men's arrest.
10. Isaac Farrer, curate of Eggleston, in his *Sermon on the late Great Flood,* delivered on 24 November and 29 December 1771.
11. The last of the twenty-one houses at the south end collapsed on 7 December. The few left standing at the north end were beyond repair.
12. Now Church Walk.
13. *Newcastle Courant*, 27 November 1771.
14. *Travels of the Imagination,* Newcastle 1773. The Reverend James Murray, Scottish Dissenter and prolific writer, had a chapel in High Bridge where his outspoken sermons had considerable impact on local politics. It was occasionally thought advisable, in the interests of law and order, for the town's serjeants to be present.
15. John Smeaton (1724—1792) had already directed a number of projects in the north. His only bridge, over the Tyne at Hexham, was completed in 1777 but was swept away in 1782, after severe flooding, owing to the defective foundations of the piers.

    Robert Mylne (1734–1811) was the engineer for Blackfriars Bridge, London. Begun in 1760 it had 9 elliptical arches—the first in England—and was built on the caisson principle. He was later appointed surveyor of St. Paul's Cathedral.
16. On this occasion the cost worked out at 1s. 0½d. per foot, exclusive of the 3s. 4d. paid to the town piper to enliven the workmen's labours.
17. Common Council minutes, 25 February, 17 March, 27 May 1772.
18. Father of David Stephenson, architect for All Saints' Church.
19. *Newcastle Courant*, 29 April 1775.
20. Officially opened 16 January 1850. Robert Stephenson was the chief engineer.

2

FOUR MATHEMATICIANS

As the eighteenth century advanced, the corresponding expansion of heavy industries in the North-East depended in ever greater measure on mathematical skills. The region was therefore fortunate in producing several mathematicians, who put their knowledge and ability to impart that knowledge at the disposal of their fellow-northerners and of the country at large.

The lives of four local mathematicians—Lionel Charlton, George Coughron, William Emerson and Charles Hutton—reveal a stimulating divergence of character, attainments and ancillary interests.

The register of Bellingham parish church records the baptism on 22 December 1720, of Lionel son of Peter Charlton of Upper Stobbilee.[1] He was severely handicapped by lameness and a withered hand, which prevented him from carrying on the farming tradition of his family. Instead his parents sent him to Edinburgh University, with a view to entering either the ministry or the teaching profession. His mathematical interests inclined him towards the latter, and he returned home after his university career, in which he distinguished himself in mathematics and Latin, full of enthusiasm for establishing a local school. His school, however, failed to prosper, either from lack of local interest, or from the fact that as a teacher, he was generally considered strict to the point of severity.

Discouraged by his lack of success, Charlton determined to seek his fortune elsewhere. He had friends in Whitby and,

Whitby Bay. From an old engraving

hoping to find there a wider scope for his abilities he arrived in 1748, complete with a strong North Country accent which he never lost. Whitby proved considerably more appreciative of his scholastic attainments than had his native Northumberland. His school, which he opened in the Tollbooth, was for a long time the principal establishment of its kind in Whitby, and produced pupils who were later to be accounted men of note in the district.

Apart from teaching, Charlton soon became a valued contributor on mathematical subjects to the *Ladies' Diary* and *Gentleman's Diary*, with which the other mathematicians were also connected. Furthermore, he turned his knowledge of mathematics to practical account by doing some much needed land-surveying for his adopted town. None of these undertakings proved particularly lucrative, but such was Charlton's integrity that he would never accept any gratuity offered to him in excess of his stated fees. All who met Charlton praised his honesty and unaffectedness. He possessed to a marked degree the Northcountryman's sturdy independence. His pertinacity, upon occasion, degenerated into downright obstinacy. Once Charlton protested publicly and vociferously against the levying of tithes upon the local fishermen. As he refused to retract one syllable of what he had said, the bishop threatened to bring a libel action which, as he had no justifiable defence, would have proved ruinous to Charlton. Fortunately for him, the bishop died before he could implement his threat.

Both the *Local Records* and the *Gentleman's Magazine*, in its 'Obituary of Considerable Persons,' refer to Charlton primarily as a mathematician. He had, however, another overriding interest for which he eventually abandoned his mathematical studies. That was the study of antiquities. As early as 1753 he had published in the *Gentleman's Magazine* a description of Roman antiquities noted at Risingham during a visit to his native valley, and towards the end of his life, he embarked upon his *History of Whitby*, the first to be published, and which Gough considered worthy of mention in his *British Topography* (1780).

An interest in history seems to be no uncommon thing among mathematicians of greater and lesser repute. The most interesting part of Charles Hutton's *Mathematical Tables* is the extensive and erudite introduction which contains a detailed and impartial historical account of early trigonometrical writings. He wrote, too, a *History of Algebra.* The later years of Sir Isaac Newton's life were also occupied with a similar interest. Newton had often read history and chronology as a mental relaxation, and his *Chronology of Ancient Kingdoms* was finished only a short time before his death in 1727, and published in the following year. It would seem, therefore, that the main criticism levelled against Charton's *History of Whitby*—that it was written in order of time only, and gave no connected view of any one subject, no correlation of cause and effect—can be countered by the fact that a mathematician naturally prefers the chronological treatment of events. In any case, Charlton very neatly disarmed this criticism by remarking in his preface:

Whatever faults may be espied by the critics in the following sheets, must entirely be imputed to my want of abilities, and the not knowing how to digest the several particulars contained therein more properly.

This work, which appeared in 1779, had become scarce by 1817, but it served its immediate purpose, which was to awaken the attention of the people of Whitby to the richness of the history and antiquities of the town and neighbourhood. Its fame spread far beyond Whitby. Copies were ordered from such widely distant places as Memel and Madrid. Among the subscribers were Dr. Samuel Johnson and Sir Joshua Reynolds, while North Shields alone accounted for fully one eighth of the issue.

The reason for this is fairly obvious. According to Charlton, and to the later historian of Whitby, Dr. George Young, the Tyne colliers practically financed the building of Whitby piers.

At the end of the seventeenth century Whitby piers were so inadequate that no heavily laden vessels could enter the harbour. The result was an appalling loss of life in stormy weather, and, during the reign of King William, the capture of many ships by His Majesty's enemies within sight of Whitby itself. Charlton says:

Moved with these considerations, the parliament of England, in the year 1702, passed an act, whereby all ships—that should load or ship any coals at the port of Newcastle-upon-Tyne, or at Sunderland, Blithe, Seaton-Sluice, Cullercoats, or any other place reputed to be a member of the said port of Newcastle-upon-Tyne, after the first of May, 1702, for a term of nine years thence next ensuing, were made liable to pay one farthing per chauldron for the same, towards repairing and rebuilding the piers belonging to the town of Whitby: And for every chauldron of coals, landed within the haven or piers of the said port of Whitby, sixpence—Likewise every English ship or vessel, which should enter the piers of the said port, was to pay one shilling, and moreover, four pence for each of her tops.

Admittedly foreign ships had to pay heavier dues, and there was a proviso that, if an adequate sum was raised within the nine years, the duty of one farthing per chaldron upon coals was to cease. The adequate sum was not forthcoming and in 1709, 1720 and 1735, Parliament obligingly passed similar acts, all of which weighed heavily upon the Tyne colliers. In 1750, far from seeing the work completed, the trustees found themselves in debt to the extent of £6,200, and a similar appeal, equally successful, was again made to Parliament. The debt continued to mount, and soon assumed the alarming proportions of £11,700, with the result that these burdensome dues were continued, by Act of Parliament, until 1797.

Charlton remains discreetly quiet about Tyneside's reactions to the situtation, and about the price Whitby was forced to pay for her coal. Evidently we still made a reasonable profit from our transactions, for Charlton writes in 1776:

> 16,000 chaldron[2] of coals are yearly brought into our port from Sunderland, Newcastle, and Blyth-Nook; somewhat more than the half of which are consumed in the town of Whitby, and the remainder either used at the allum-works, or consumed in the country adjacent.

A man of integrity, a mathematician and classical scholar of no mean attainments, Charlton died at Whitby in 1788. If he found no fame in his native valley, Dr. Young, despite his strictures on Charlton's historical work, considered him worthy to be chronicled with such eminent natives of Whitby as the Chapmans, who later came to Newcastle, and founded the Willington Ropery, the Chaloners, the Cholmleys and the famous Captain Cook.

In 1752, at Wreigh-hill, under the shadow of Simonside, there was born to John Coughron, farmer, a third son, George. His father confidently assumed that the boy would in due course take his share in farming the land which had been in the family for generations. As soon as his schooldays were over, he was set his allotted tasks of ploughing and working about the barns and byres. His heart, however, was clearly not in his work, and every hour that he could snatch from work or sleep was devoted to the study of mathematics, in which he was practically self-taught, for the village school-master early declared that he could no longer pretend to teach a pupil who had already far outstripped him. There is indeed a probability that George Coughron had, before he was eighteen, opened a small school of his own, thus following in the footsteps of Milton and Dr. Johnson, who, from such humble beginnings, rose to fame. At all events, Coughron, in his poem *Farewell to Coquetdale*, wrote:

Farewell to all who did my school frequent;
May your desire on learning still be bent!
Were you aware how it might you advance,
You would it prize and hate all ignorance.

The first public proof of Coughron's budding mathematical genius appeared in the columns of the *Newcastle Courant*. This paper was in the habit of offering its readers mathematical problems, and Coughron's answer was on one occasion published as the clearest and best received. Encouraged by this success, Coughron submitted a problem of his own for solution. It was sent, not in his own name, but in that of his great friend, William Wilkin, another self-taught mathematician of Alnwick. Further problems and solutions were contributed to the *Courant* by Coughron, some of which displayed remarkable ability and ingenuity, and it soon became known locally that these anonymous efforts were the work of the young son of a Rothbury farmer.

Shortly afterwards the proprietors of the *British Oracle* sponsored a mathematical competition, open to all England, and Coughron carried off the silver medal awarded to the successful competitor. His fame now spread far beyond Coquetdale. Every mathematician of repute in the country was aware that a new mathematical genius was in the making.

His father who, up to this point, had doggedly cherished hopes of turning his son into an enthusiastic farmer, now found himself forced to abandon all such thoughts, and to let his young son follow his own bent. In 1770 George Coughron left Wreigh-hill for Newcastle. He celebrated his departure in a poem of some hundred lines, *Farewell to Coquetdale*. It would seem that a love of mathematics and poetry is less common than a love of mathematics and history. Still more rarely does a man reach great heights in both spheres. Coughron, if he was not a poetical genius, at least had ability above the average. His little poem, simple and sincere in expression, reflects his own honest and unaffected character, his warm friendship and generous sympathies, his unfeigned desire for the welfare of all about him, his deep affection for his family and birth-place. Among his friends he numbered members of many well-known local families, the Donkins, Storeys, Ramsays and Robsons, of whom he speaks in the most affectionate terms. He is particularly anxious for the welfare of one brother

Whose genius great and lofty muse should be
In books recorded to futurity;
For every science and each liberal art
Proclaims you master of a noble part.
Much I lament whene'er I think upon
Your fate, thus buried in oblivion:
O! that you would procure some worthy friend,
Who could promote you to a noble end,
In which you might advance, and leave the plough
To such as nothing better seek to know.

As far as can be ascertained, this brother lived and died unknown in Coquetdale. The lines penned by the youthful Coughron are strongly reminiscent of the passage in Gray's *Elegy written in a Country Churchyard:*

Perhaps in this neglected spot is laid
  Some heart once pregnant with celestial fire;
Hands, that the rod of empire might have sway'd,
  Or waked to extasy the living lyre:
But knowledge to their eyes her ample page
  Rich with the spoils of time, did ne'er unroll;
Chill penury repress'd their noble rage,
  And froze the genial current of the soul.

Two further points in Coughron's poem are worthy of notice —his insistence upon his complete and final severance from his childhood's home, and his reference to that foreordained time

When the pale King of terrors draweth nigh,
  And we have nothing more to do, but die.

Had Coughron even then some premonition of what Fate held in store for him?

A tall, slim youth, fair-haired and fair-complexioned, Coughron, at the age of eighteen, came to Newcastle and lodged in Broad Chare, near the great mathematical school of Trinity House. He became a clerk with Brown, the wine and spirit merchant at the Head of the Side. The offices faced Joseph Barber's famous circulating library and were not far from William Charnley's establishment. Subscription libraries were a comparatively recent innovation in England. The first was established by Samuel Fancourt at Salisbury in 1740, and it appears to be to Barber's credit that he opened the first in Newcastle. His rival Charnley, opened another library in the Flesh Market in 1757. Both libraries were very well stocked with English and foreign books on history, literature, divinity, geography, mathematics. Among the latter there appeared, as they were published, the works of Emerson and Hutton. Barber and Charnley were themselves well-read men of wide interests and forceful personalities. The former was a fluent talker, a classical scholar, conversant with spoken and written French, and well acquainted with *belles-lettres*. The latter was highly respected in Newcastle for his accurate and extensive knowledge of books, his integrity and generosity, his interest in the welfare of the town and for his work in connection with the establishment and early management of the Literary and Philosophical Society. Those who strolled into the libraries on market days might hear, as the chimes of St. Nicholas marked the quarter hours, the proprietors discussing with their patrons the lastest volumes of Hume, Sterne, Johnson and Adam Smith, or the latest news from the local press. Among their patrons were all the well-informed men of the district, including Dr. Brown, the Vicar of Newcastle, his successor, Dr. Fawcett, Matthew Ridley and his son, both of whom so frequently represented Newcastle in Parliament, Edward Montague of Denton Hall, that 'gay Lothario,' Sir Frances Blake Delaval, Hugh Moises, headmaster of the Free Grammar School, Aubone Surtees the banker, Thomas Bewick the engraver, John Cunningham the poet, and Charles Hutton the mathematician. Such was the congenial *milieu* into which Coughron had the good fortune to be introduced.

Almost immediately Coughron and Hutton struck up a friendship. At the time the latter was extremely busy with his

The Flesh Market, Newcastle, in 1772

school and private pupils, the writing of books and the preparation of a survey of the town, undertaken at the request of the Corporation. He was also engaged upon a reprint of what he called the 'useful' parts of the *Ladies' Diary*, to which, like Coughron, he was himself a frequent contributor. Coughron collaborated with Hutton in this undertaking, but it appears that this partnership was short-lived. Some suggest that the breach was caused by a financial misunderstanding. Others that Hutton was jealous of Coughron's fame. The latter suggestion is highly improbable. Hutton was already well-known as a teacher of repute and a writer on mathematical subjects, while his talents were, within a year, to secure for him the post of professor of mathematics at the Royal Military Academy at Woolwich. It seems more likely that the disparity in their ages—Hutton was thirty-five and Coughron only twenty—was responsible for a natural divergence in views and a consequent coolness in their relations.

About this time, two eminent mathematicians, Maskelyne the Astronomer-Royal and Heath, author of the *British Palladium*, had a difference of opinion which they decided to settle by the mediation of some third, competent party. Both were acquainted with Coughron's name and reputation in the mathematical world, but were apparently unaware of his age and modest status. Coughron decided in favour of Heath, and his friends warned him that, by failing to support the Astronomer-Royal, he had destroyed his chances of advancement. Their fears proved groundless, for soon afterwards a member of the staff of Greenwich Observatory was sent by Maskelyne to interview Coughron. The gentleman stood amazed at the sight of such a young man and then exclaimed: 'God bless my soul—a child!' Nevertheless, the 'child,' as a result of the interview, was engaged on very liberal terms to be calculator to the Astronomer-Royal.

Heath, whose point of view he had so firmly upheld, was also loud in his praises. 'All those who wish to wear laurels,' he wrote, 'should win them like Mr. George Coughron, to whom nothing appears too difficult for his penetration to accomplish.' Coughron justified Heath's belief in him by challenging any mathematician to solve a most difficult question in the *Gentleman's Diary* (1772) and, as no one produced a solution, by himself providing the answer. Some ten prizes were also awarded to him for his work on fluxions alone, which caused one mature rival mathematician, the Reverend Charles Wildbore, to retire from the contest with the 'sapling sage' as he appropriately dubbed him.

The 'sapling', flourishing though it appeared to be, was not to be allowed to grow to maturity. In 1774 George Coughron, when on the threshold of a promising career, was carried off by the scourge of small-pox. John Brand, the local historian, conducted the burial service in Saint Andrew's Churchyard, and entered in the register a few brief words which epitomize Coughron's character and career.

1774. January 10th, George Coughron, gentleman, an eminent mathematician.

They will have little to do, I think, that set about writing my life: I am sure of this, half of it will be lies; therefore I chuse to die in the same obscurity I have lived.

Such was the typically uncompromising attitude of William Emerson towards his would-be biographer. In his long life (1701–1782) he proved himself to be a mathematician of outstanding attainments, an original character, lovable despite all his weaknesses, and biographers have wisely ignored his ban.

The son of a small landowner and schoolmaster of Hurworth near Darlington, Emerson, for the first twenty years of his life, showed a greater love of sport than of knowledge and must have been something of a trial to his father, who was responsible for his general education, and to the young curate, who undertook to teach him Greek and Latin. His keen and penetrating eye, his eager expression, indicated an active mind, and eventually he became alive to the attractions of science. Full of enthusiasm, he studied under the ablest masters he could find in York and Newcastle, where he formed a lifelong friendship with Robert Harrison, headmaster of the Trinity House School. On returning to Hurworth, he tried his hand at teaching, but with small success, and for two reasons. Both then, and in his published works, his demonstrations were too concise for the average student, and he did not suffer fools gladly. Patience was never one of Emerson's virtues. An amusing, if unauthenticated tale clearly proves this point.

John Hunter, a bricklayer, pupil and friend of Emerson, was one day repairing the roof of Emerson's house, while the owner stood below preparing the lime and mortar. A post-chaise drew up and out stepped a deputation from Cambridge University with an abstruse problem, which they hoped the great Mr. Emerson would solve. 'Great or little, I am the man,' remarked Emerson with characteristic brusqueness, as the gentlemen, rather pardonably, failed to identify the eminent mathematician in the bricklayer's mate. Emerson glanced at the problem, and then shouted: 'John Hunter, come down, and do thou answer this!' Hunter duly got down from the roof and, after a few minutes' silent calculation, wrote the answer in chalk on the crown of his hat. With some difficulty the deputation prevailed upon Emerson to check the result, and then professed themselves unable to understand the solution, whereupon Emerson testily remarked: 'Take the hat home—and return it when you have discovered the explanation!'

On another occasion Emerson was invited to appear before a committee of the House of Commons to give advice on the construction of one of the earliest stone bridges across the Thames. The committee waited long and in vain for the expert's appearance. A harassed messenger eventually discovered him striding back to Hurworth—he always walked to and from London—and adamant in his refusal to return to Westminster. Perhaps Emerson's lack of interest was due to the very poor opinion he had of British bridge-builders. He says in his *Tract on Mechanics:*

I had taken a great deal of pains, to find out the true form of a bridge, that shall be the strongest, and of a ship that shall sail the fastest;—But, as we have no occasion in England for the strongest bridges or the swiftest ships, Mathematicians, for the future, may find something else to do, than run into such perplext and useless disquisitions. For indeed when any of these grand things are to be performed, they generally fall into the hands of such people, as know little of the nature of them—but in this there is no great wonder, considering how few people study this art; and among those that do, how few are competent judges.

It is not surprising that Emerson never reaped any material advantages from his undoubtedly valuable contributions to the mathematical sciences. Moreover, if any reward had been offered him, it is highly improbable that he would have accepted it. Of the honour of Fellowship of the Royal Society, he once remarked:

It was a d——d hard thing that a man should burn so many farthing candles as he had done, and then have to pay so much a year for the honour of F.R.S. after his name; d——n them, and their F.R.S. too!

William Emerson

Emerson seems to have thought that wordly success automatically turned a man's head. He it was who advised Hutton to make his successful application for the post at the Royal Military Academy. Yet, in 1774, he writes—'I never had a line from Hutton; his good luck makes him forget his old friends,' and five years later, 'I must tell him likewise that I am a mere volunteer in the service, having no large salaries or premiums from the public, and am in no way accountable to them. So that I stand no chance of being turn'd out of office for malpractice.'

It is to Hutton's credit that he bore Emerson no ill-will for this churlish attitude. Hutton's account of him in his *Mathematical and Philosophical Dictionary* is absolutely unbiassed. He praises Emerson's vigour of mind, his deep knowledge, theoretical and practical, of all branches of mathematics and physics, the soundness of his published works. In his *History of Algebra* he gives due prominence to Emerson's *Increments* and *Algebra*. The one adverse criticism he makes of Emerson, that 'he could discourse sensibly on any subject, but was always positive and impatient of any contradiction,' was undeniably true.

Eccentric in character, Emerson was equally eccentric in dress and manners. Sartorial fashions were a matter of complete indifference to him. Comfort was his sole criterion. His linen, spun and bleached by his wife, was chosen for its warmth and durability, and he was frequently known to wear his shirt back to front in cold weather as a chest protector. He generally affected a wide-brimmed hat. When the brim, through sheer old age, began to droop disconsolately over his eyes, he would seize a pair of scissors and rapidly trim the offending headgear into a rough and ready jockey's cap. When he grew older and sat by a roaring winter's fire, he protected his legs with old sacking covers, tied round the knees with string. These he alluded to as his 'shin-covers,' and they have gained immortality in the writings of Thomas Carlyle. Emerson made his own wigs out of flax. They never saw a brush or comb, and as he had a habit of poking his hand up the back whenever he was perplexed, they rarely fulfilled their original purpose of covering his scanty grey locks, but hung rakishly over one eye.

His diet was as simple and plain as his dress. Meals were never allowed to interfere with his studies or amusements. He seldom sat down to eat, but would take a huge piece of cold pie into his study and satisfy, as he used to say, his appetite for food and knowledge at the same time. Emerson did his own marketing and visited Darlington each Monday for the purpose. He frequently failed to return home before the Tuesday or Wednesday, having spent the time in the local inns, sustaining lively arguments and discussions on all manner of subjects, mechanics, religion and politics. His last visit to Darlington was in the nature of a triumphal progress. He rode in solemn state upon a sorry nag, whose intrinsic value, according to his biographers, was half a crown and maximum speed one and a half miles per hour. A neighbour begged the honour of his company on the return journey. 'Thou fool, thou!' said Emerson. 'Thou'll be at home long enough before me, man. Thou walks, and I ride!'

His peculiar mannerisms, combined with his reputation

for profound learning, caused Emerson to be considered a magician by the illiterate. They would come to him to find stolen goods for them or to reveal the hidden secrets of the future, but the supposed prophet treated all enquirers with scant patience. He was popularly supposed to have kept a would-be despoiler of his orchard pinned by a magic spell to the top of a tree, where he was forced to spend a whole Sunday morning in full view of the congregation wending its way to and from church. That he did compel a man to sit for hours in a fruit tree was a fact. The method he employed was severely practical. He stood, hatchet in hand, at the foot of the tree and swore he would hew the man's legs off if he came down.

Others accused Emerson of atheism. He was as much an atheist as he was a magician. His wife was the niece of the Rector of Hurworth, who had promised her a dowry of £500, but did not choose to honour his promise. The pecuniary loss troubled Emerson not at all, as he had modest means of his own, but the Rector treated him as a person of no consequence, entirely beneath his notice, and that Emerson would not brook. His quarrel, therefore, was with the priest, rather than the priesthood. Smarting under the Rector's treatment he set to work to examine the Old and New Testaments, and gleefully compiled two small volumes of what he considered to be contradictory passages. These he arranged like hostile troops on the opposite pages of his book, termed by a contemporary critic 'pitiful cavils against the consistency of the holy scriptures.' He may have been influenced at the time by the theological writing of Sir Isaac Newton, whose staunch supporter he was to become. Newton, it will be remembered, had been accused of Anti-Trinitarianism. A man who is wholly engaged in a science which admits of demonstrable proofs at every step, may have greater difficulty than others in accepting matters of faith. Emerson, though on occasion he may have spoken lightly of revealed religion, of the established church, and of the clergy, himself said that he firmly believed in the existence of a God; he did not only believe it, he knew it; he was certain of it to a demonstration.

Mention has already been made of Hutton's comment upon Emerson's practical work, which was not entirely devoted to scientific subjects. He was greatly interested in music in so far as it depends upon mathematical and philosophical principles. Although a poor performer, he was skilled in the theory of sounds, the various scales, and the construction of a wide range of musical instruments from the bagpipes to the organ. Nothing pleased him better than to go round the countryside tuning his neighbours' harpsichords, and he often put his mathematical speculations into practice by constructing a variety of musical instruments and adding what he hoped would be improvements to those already in existence. He added an extra string to his violin to make the E more melodious, and introduced additional half-tones to his virginal, in an attempt to rectify some fraction of discord that always remained after tuning. This he could never regulate to his satisfaction, and generally ended by muttering irascibly, 'It is a d——d instrument, and a foolish thing to be vexed with.' His exasperation over an ill-tuned virginal was counterbalanced by his exemplary patience when fishing. A keen angler, he would stand for hours up to his waist in water for he scorned the use of a boat. He did indeed build himself a small boat when he was busy with his *Treatise on Navigation* (1755), and he and some young friends embarked in it for testing on the Tees. As a practical demonstration of the treatise the vessel was a failure, but the pleasure derived from the outings increased in proportion to the number of times that the amateur crew was swamped.

Apart from contributions to the *Ladies' Diary* under the anagram *Merones*, Emerson did no serious writing until he was over forty. Then for more than thirty years he produced an unbroken succession of books on every aspect of mathematics and physics, of which the best known are his *Mechanics* and *Method of Increments*. He always revised the proofs of his books himself, his favourite maxim being 'to trust no eyes but his own,' and any criticism of his work roused him to a frenzy of indignation. Emerson was well-read, had a good command of words, and sufficient mental vigour to give weight to what he wrote. In conversation, however, he was generally very abrupt and blunt, and critics were apt to judge the written by the spoken word. On being told that most people considered his prefaces were not his own composition, he exclaimed: 'A pack of fools! Who could write my prefaces but myself?' and indeed, the original prefaces and manuscripts of his works were then in the hands of the publishers. Emerson waxed even more indignant at criticism of the actual matter of his writings. Through a mutual friend[3] he had many an acrimonious argument with Hutton, who had accused him, probably with reason, of receiving with evident ill-humour his well-meant hints. This, according to Emerson, was a most scandalous falsehood and pure detraction. Though he bitterly resented criticism of his own work, Emerson would write of another author: 'This article is nothing but empty harangue. . . . for shame to write such stuff as this,' while, in the preface to his *Miscellanies,* he wrote:

> I cannot dismiss this affair, without taking notice of a certain obscure Critic, who insulted and abused me in the *Gentleman's Magazine,* for some trifling numerical errors in the Astronomy, that any body, with the least smattering of Mathematics, might rectify. Yet this DRAWCANSIR kept barking at me out of his hole, in several of the Magazines, and pretended to criticize my Book, though he acknowledged he did not understand it. A fine sort of Critic, indeed, to rail at me for his own dullness.

And Emerson wound up his attack by calling the offending critic 'a little paltry School-master, an envious, abusive, dirty Scribbler.' With such a command of invective, Emerson scarcely had cause to complain of the mild criticisms levelled against himself.

Emerson's devotion to the Newtonian philosophy was so strong that every oponent of that great man was treated by him as 'dull, blind, bigoted, prejudiced, or mad.' Much as the more restrained Newton might have deprecated Emerson's abusive style, the latter did a great deal to further Newton's cause in the eighteenth century, by the publication of his *Theory of Increments*, his original translation of some of Newton's work, and his impassioned defence of the *Principia*. Newton's *Principia*, one of the greatest works on exact science ever written, marked by a simplicity of expression and sanity of outlook, had been reprinted 1739–1742, just when Emerson was embarking upon his career as a mathematician. Although Newton's teaching was early adopted at Cambridge, St. Andrews and Edinburgh, his followers remained numerically small. The Cartesian system of vortices was well entrenched and the *Principia* itself was no easy reading. Commentaries therefore became necessary, and Emerson's *Short Comment on Sir Isaac Newton's Principia* (1770) is specially mentioned among those of importance produced during the eighteenth century. Hutton, too, added his quota of praise to Emerson's work in facilitating and spreading the doctrine of fluxions. Emerson did not live to read what Hutton said of his work in connection with the Newtonian philosophy. Had he done so, it is doubtful whether he would have been at all appreciative for, during his lifetime, he continually cavilled at Hutton's interpretation of Newton's theories.

Towards the end of his life Emerson suffered considerable physical pain, and was often heard to wish that 'the soul might have shaken off its rags of mortality without such a clitter-me-clatter.' His usual spirits animated him to the end. Shortly before his death, he disposed of his well-stocked library to a bookseller at York. When asked why he had done so, he retorted that he had only a pack of fools to leave his books to, and money would be of more service to them than books. The inscription on his tombstone in Hurworth churchyard was typical of the man.

That which lies buried and neglected under your feet was once William Emerson, a man of primitive simplicity, the utmost integrity, the rarest genius, a consummate mathematician. If you have read his writings, to what intent speaks this stone? If you have not read them, read them that you may know.

Charles Hutton, LL.D., F.R.S.

Charles Hutton, LL.D., F.R.S., and member of several other learned societies, was the youngest son of Henry and Eleanor Hutton, born in Percy Street in 1737. His father, who died in 1742, was deputy-overman at Benton Colliery, and his brothers were all miners. Hutton himself injured his elbow in a childish quarrel at the age of seven, and did not tell his mother of the accident until the damage was beyond repair. Work in the mines seemed out of the question for him, so he was sent to school to become 'a good scholar,' as his mother put it. She could scarcely have anticipated at that time what a good scholar her young son was to become. His first teacher was an old Scotswoman, who lived at the corner of Percy Street and Gallowgate, and he remained in her charge until he had read the Bible through two or three times. On Hutton's own showing, this schoolmistress was not very well qualified, as it was her custom, whenever she came to a word which she could not read herself, to tell the children to skip it, for it was Latin. Hutton was then sent to Robson's school at Benwell, where he learned to write, and, after his mother and step-father removed to High Heaton, he attended Mr. Ivison's school at Jesmond. Here he was taught arithmetic and was first introduced to his life-long passion, mathematics. He acquired another interest, too, which remained with him always—a love of book-collecting and of reading of every description, but particularly Border ballads, tales and legends.

There now comes a gap in our knowledge of Hutton's life. In 1755 and 1756 his name appears on the paysheets of Benton Colliery, where he was employed as hewer. He was on piece work and evidently handicapped by his damaged arm, for his name comes at the bottom of the list with a very small wage beside it. About this time Mr. Ivison, who had taken a great interest in his pupil, and continued to teach him advanced mathematics, became curate at Whitburn. He therefore transferred his school to Hutton, who reopened in larger premises at Stott's or Stote's Hall, while attending James's evening classes in mathematics. James retired some four years later, and Hutton stepped into his shoes. The new school was at the head of the Flesh Market, and offered a very ambitious syllabus—writing, arithmetic, algebra, geometry, trigonometry, conics, mechanics, together with their application in navigation, surveying, gunnery, astronomy—to quote only a few subjects from his extensive list. He also offered to give private lessons in their own homes to ladies and gentlemen. This was an unusual opportunity for the gentle sex of those days. His friends advised him to be more moderate in his claims, lest his performance fall short of his promises. They were also doubtful about the wisdom of charging double the

Darlington, from the East

accepted fees, but their warning was not needed. The school flourished, and attracted many famous scholars. Among them were John Scott and Bessie Surtees, afterwards Lord and Lady Eldon. Sixty years later, Lord Eldon wrote to Lieutenant-General Henry Hutton, who was Hutton's son by his first marriage:

Full sixty years have passed since I had the benefit of your venerable father's instructions, and that benefit I regard as one of the many blessings which I have enjoyed in life, and of which blessings I wish I had been worthy. . . . He will long be remembered by a country so essentially benefited by his life and works.

This is probably the first recorded case of the indebtedness of a Lord Chancellor of England to a miner's son.

In addition to his teaching, Hutton was also becoming known as a writer on mathematical subjects. He brought out a highly successful *Practical Arithmetic* which, thanks to its clearness, precision and simplicity, was a standard text-book for generations. The book was published in Newcastle, and, to supply the want of proper mathematical types, the author was forced to cut many of them with a penknife on the reversed end of existing types. In 1770 he dedicated to the Duke of Northumberland his *Treatise on Mensuration*, the most complete and up-to-date for years to come. For the diagrams Hutton decided upon woodcuts instead of the usual steel engravings, and he enlisted the services of Bewick who had already successfully tried his apprentice hand on the illustrations for the *Ladies' Diary*, edited by Hutton. His master Beilby had put the finishing touches to this work; now Bewick worked alone. Hutton, he says:

> frequently came into the room in which I worked, to inspect what I was doing. He was always very civil, but seemed to me to be of a grave or shy deportment. He lived in habits of intimacy with my master, and used to write designs for him to engrave from, particularly for the heads of invoices or bills of parcels; and I remember that he wrote them with an ink or preparation, which was easily transferred to the copper. This was before his appointment in the Royal Military Academy of Woolwich, in 1773, and long before he had the well-merited title of LL.D. added to his respected name. Dr. Hutton was that kind of man who never forgot old friends; and some years after, when I was in partnership with my old master, he recommended us to the notice of Dr. Horsley, who was commencing his publication of Sir Isaac Newton's works, the execution of the whole of the cuts for which devolved upon me.

Hutton, it may be said, was an enthusiastic Newtonian. In his *Mathematical and Philosophical Dictionary* (1796), he devoted an article of some 18,000 words to Newton alone, and in his *Treatise on Mensuration* gave high praise to his method of fluxions, established upon principles 'free from the imperfections and absurdities attending some that had lately been introduced by the moderns.'

The *Treatise on Mensuration* called forth from a Shropshire reader a lengthy poetic eulogy which, though written over two hundred years ago, sounds a modern note.

O Science! trade and commerce are thy end,
By thee we import, and by thee we vend;
By thee we build our houses, till our lands,
And weigh and measure with unerring hands.
What art or rules could never yet display,
Nor all the rules of Science till this day
Were able to disclose be genius' force,
Thy true-born son hath traced to the Source.

Mention has already been made of Emerson's *Mechanics*, and of his exceedingly poor opinion of contemporary bridge builders, expressed both in that work and by his cavalier treatment of the parliamentary committee. About thirty years later, Hutton voiced very similar sentiments. In 1771, a spring flood, which rose about eight feet above the normal level, played havoc with the bridges over the Tyne, of which the only one left standing was that at Corbridge on the old Roman foundation. The following year saw the publication of Hutton's *Principles of Bridges*, and we gather from it that bridge builders had failed to profit from Emerson's words of wisdom. 'A large and elegant bridge,' says Hutton, 'forming a way over a broad and rapid river, is justly esteemed one of the noblest pieces of mechanism that man is capable of performing,' and he was anxious that the new bridge over the Tyne at Newcastle should be a credit to the town. But, he continues:

This occasion having furnished me with many opportunities of hearing and seeing very absurd things advanced on the subject in general, I thought the demonstration of the relations of the essential parts of a bridge would not be unacceptable to those architects and others who may be capable of perceiving the force of them, and whose ignorance may not have prejudiced them against things which they do not understand.

To round off the parallel with Emerson, the *Principles of*

Bridges was republished in the early nineteenth century when the author's advice was asked on the rebuilding of London Bridge.

The time had come for Hutton to bid farewell to Newcastle. He often planned to revisit the North and even in his eighty-fifth year he wrote:

> If health permit me, I fully intend to do myself the honour and great pleasure of accomplishing in summer my pilgrimage to the dear place of my nativity . . . I was honoured with a visit from Sir John Swinburne, the worthy president of your Literary and Philosophical Society . . . He was also so kind as to solicit my visit to Newcastle, and kindly recommended the same easy mode of conveyance that you mention (this was the London and Leith steam packet, which would have landed him at Tynemouth) and which indeed is the only one which I could venture to encounter; for I well remember that in my youth, more than half a century ago, I was almost shaken to pieces by land conveyance, in two or three journeys then made to London.

Hutton died the following year, his journey unaccomplished, but all his life he kept in close contact with Newcastle, and proved a very generous benefactor to three local institutions, the Royal Jubilee School, the Schoolmasters' Association, established in 1774 for the support of aged and infirm members and their widows, and the Literary and Philosophical Association, of which he was elected an honorary member and whose gradual expansion he encouraged by practical and sympathetic support. In 1822 the Society fixed on a permanent site, and Hutton gave a subscription of £20 towards the new building which would be, he wrote:

> so central and convenient, and so near to the last abode of myself. I know the house well, and have often seen it; and which, when I left Newcastle, was, and had been for many years before, the residence of Mr. Gibson, the Town Clerk . . . . The house was always esteemed a very excellent one, with a fine open area in front, and spacious garden behind, extending to the Town Walls.

This building was later to house the bust of Hutton, subscribed for as a mark of respect and veneration for one who, as author and teacher, had done so much to advance mathematical and scientific studies.

His greatest sphere of influence as a teacher was his professorship at the Royal Military Academy, which he held for more than forty years. Hutton secured this post entirely on his own merits, in a competitive examination in which he far outstripped his ten rivals. The examiners, who included Dr. Horsley, the learned editor of Newton's works, and Dr. Maskelyne, the Astronomer-Royal, were unanimous in their decision, the wisdom of which soon became fully apparent. By his prompt and unfailing attendance to his duties, by the books he wrote for use in the Academy, by the experiments he conducted for the improvement of gunnery, Hutton raised the standard of mathematical teaching at the Academy and turned out a number of highly qualified officers. As a lecturer, he was deliberate and clear, his illustrations were apt and convincing, his experiments neat and successful, while he showed unlimited patience and perseverance in explaining any difficulties under which his students laboured. The Academy also shone in the reflected glory of his fellowship of the Royal Society, of which he was for some time foreign secretary, and his learned contributions to the *Philosophical Transactions*, some of which earned him the annual gold medal, and were said to have been the most valuable since the days of Newton. A proof of the value of his paper on the *Force of Exploded Gunpowder* is given by Delambre in his life of Lagrange. At the height of the French Revolution, foreigners were ordered to leave France. This edict applied to Lagrange, an Italian by birth, despite his name, but he was allowed to remain, as he was engaged on experiments of the utmost importance to the country, experiments based upon Hutton's report. It would have been interesting to know the outcome of Lagrange's researches but they are lost in oblivion.

Upon his resignation from Woolwich, due to ill-health, Hutton took a house in Bedford Row, London, where he devoted himself to revising and reprinting his now formidable list of works. As a writer he was highly popular and he was for long accepted as the standard author upon mathematical subjects. His treatises had the great merit of being clearly and logically expressed, whilst avoiding those digressions so often indulged in by writers who are anxious to show how much they know of subjects other than those under immediate discussion. Hutton's works are not all serious. The great man had his lighter moments, and in 1814, brought out an improved translation of Ozonam's *Recreations in Mathematics and Natural Philosophy*. Ozonam had a dry sense of humour. Refusing to be drawn into the theological discussions of his day, he remarked that 'it was the business of the Sorbonne doctors to discuss, of the Pope to decide, and of a *Mathematician to go straight to heaven in a perpendicular line.*' The italics are Hutton's. The *Recreations* would delight the heart of the average small boy. In it are to be found card tricks, the usual mathematical problems of the goat, wolf and cabbage variety with an entertaining variant, wherein three jealous husbands are confronted with the task of ferrying their wives across a river. There is no boatman, the boat holds only two passengers. How then is the crossing to be effected in such a way that no woman is left in the company of the other men unless her husband is present? There are recipes for making invisible inks, and a method of making an artificial volcano, which would probably prove a source of great entertainment for a young geographer and of corresponding irritation for his parents.

The London papers of 1815 record an elaborate hoax played upon Hutton. Evidently the anonymous perpetrator thought Hutton's sense of humour sufficiently strong to stand the strain. Some mischievous wag summoned by post about half the tradesmen in London to wait upon Dr. Hutton with their various wares.

At an early hour in the morning, (so runs one account), the family were accordingly disturbed by the arrival of a hearse and two horses, with mourning coaches to correspond. Shortly afterwards, an elegant post-chaise drove up—the horses and postillions were decorated with favours as if to carry into the country a new married couple. Next came a post-chaise and four with the same decorations. Then followed several coffins, plain and ornamental—not forgetting one patent receptacle of this kind for frail mortality—Towards noon the higher classes consisting of physicians, accoucheurs, and apothecaries, in their splendid carriages, began to arrive, all summoned on the same fruitless errand. The scene, in short, continued the whole of the afternoon; for the hoax seems to have been so contrived that the mischief should afford a whole day's sport to the idle vulgar. It is impossible to enumerate the many articles of luxury and utility which were conveyed to the door in question. The coal dealers, and proprietors of post horses and chaises seem, however, to have been the chief sufferers. The coal waggons, in particular, at one time, nearly blocked up the street.

The reporter, perhaps wisely, omitted any comment on the reactions either of Dr. Hutton or the unwilling participants in this hoax.

An allusion has already been made to Hutton's practice of collecting curious and rare books. He was never content with merely reading a book, he must always have a copy of his own, with the result he collected a fine private library, with the best mathematical collection of the time in England. Hutton did not dispose of his library in such a summary fashion as Emerson. He hoped that, on his death, which occurred in 1823, it would be purchased intact for the benefit of the British Museum. His wishes were not realized, apparently owing to a longstanding private feud, and the books were auctioned. A number were bought by the Literary and Philosophical Society, and it is to be regretted that the whole collection did not come back to Newcastle, whose local press was responsible for this obituary notice: 'He was *one* among the *few* who do honour to the place of their birth, and Newcastle lays claim to that honour.'

Bewick, as well as being a famous engraver, was something of a philosopher and educationist. In his *Memoir* we find the following lines which are indeed applicable to these four mathematicians, and which, today, when equality of opportunity is the watchword, merit our careful attention and consideration.

In viewing man as connected with this world, and with his station in society, I think it will appear clearly that the various degrees of his intellectual and reasoning powers are the gift of Providence . . . . It is this innate power drawn forth and acted upon by observation and industry, that enables the philosopher, the poet, the painter, and the musician to arrive at excellence; and the same remark is more or less applicable to men bent upon any pursuit in the whole round of the arts and sciences. Without using the means to cultivate their powers, they will remain inert, and be of no use either to the individual or to society; and men with innate qualifications, and men without them are brought down to a level of uselessness. It is greatly owing to the want of effort that originates the inequalities of rank and fortune of which the community is composed.

NOTES

1. The year of his birth has been erroneously stated as 1722.
2. In 1678 the weight of a Newcastle chaldron was fixed at 53 cwt.
3. Robert Harrison.

3
TYNESIDE ENGINEERING

'WE WONDER what blockhead first built Newcastle; for, before you can get into and out of it, you must descend one hill, and ascend another about as steep as the sides of a coal-pit.'[1] Despite this and other alleged disadvantages, there were eighteenth-century engineers willing to come and settle in the district. They required none of our modern inducements, no government white papers or regional planning teams, no North East Development Council, no *Voice of North-East Industry*. They came of their own accord, tackled the same problems that face industry today—siting, production methods, recruitment of labour, relations between management and men—and they opened up the trade of one of the least industrial areas in the country.

Nowadays engineering covers a vast field of enquiry, agricultural, chemical, civil, electrical, marine, mechanical, mining, much of which was barely touched upon two hundred years ago. Electrical engineering, for example, was non-existent, the study of electricity in its infancy. The eccentric millionaire mathematician Cavendish was busy with his experiments. Gray had established (1736) that an electric current could be transmitted a considerable distance along pack-thread and Dr. Watson had completed a circuit across the Thames at Westminster Bridge. Franklin, whose account of his *Electrical Kite* appeared in 1751, saw his lightning-conductors installed on Buckingham Palace (1762) and Priestley discovered the Law of Inverse Squares in 1766. Few laymen sensed the possibility of increasing national prosperity and of a general improvement in the standard of living inherent in this new science, although Wesley advocated the application of severe electric shocks in the treatment of hysteria, a thesis in which prominent alienists, who were cautiously feeling their way towards psychiatric methods, evinced no interest whatsoever.[2] Electricity was popularly regarded as the source of a new parlour game. Audiences were highly entertained on seeing brandy ignited by a spark shooting out from a man's finger, while across the Channel, Louis XV displayed immoderate hilarity when a long line of monks leapt into the air on the application of an electric shock.

In general, eighteenth-century society frowned upon engineers. It is true that many—Brindley, Rennie, the Stephensons, Telford—were of humble origin but they had outstanding ability, a great creative urge balanced by a sense of discipline and duty; they were determined and resilient in the face of social censure and of any setback in their work caused by their empirical methods. Where new processes or new machines were involved, trial and error were, of necessity, their yardstick. Only the wealthy could afford the heavy fees for a five-year apprenticeship under a consultant engineer, and it was not until 1799, when the first technical college in the United Kingdom was opened in Glasgow, that the working-man had an opportunity of attending lectures. At first there were few text-books available, particularly in English,[3] while subscription libraries with their modest selection of technical periodicals did not appear until the end of the century. With the exception of the Royal Society (1662) whose business was 'to improve the Knowledge of naturall Things, and all useful Arts, Manufactures, Mechanick Practices, Engynes and Inventions by Experiment,' learned bodies such as the Society of Arts (1754), which dealt with new inventions, the Society of Civil Engineers (1771) and the Royal Institution (1790) were late in their inception.

For all that engineers were treated with scant respect, the benefits which their labours conferred on the public were accepted as a matter of course. They were termed military engineers when their skills served our troops at home during the Jacobite risings or abroad, in Europe, India, Canada and America, during the recurrent wars into which we were plunged. In the interludes of peace they became civil engineers but their task was the same. In either case the country required docks, harbours, roads, bridges, canals, mining and agricultural machinery. To satisfy these needs they exerted greater skill, judgement and administrative ability than an indifferent public ever realised.

The engineer who made the strongest impact upon Tyneside at the beginning of the century, Sir Ambrose Crowley (Crawley),[4] has attracted much attention of late,[5] perhaps because his worth has been so often and so differently assessed in the past two hundred years. He has been called a great patron of manufactory and trade, an enterprising genius, a benevolent despot, a semi-socialist, the Mussolini of Winlaton. Wherein does the truth lie?

That Sir Ambrose was a go-ahead and successful business man is undeniable. The son of a Quaker nailer of Stourbridge, Worcestershire, he died in 1713, aged fifty-four, an alderman of the City of London, Deputy-Governor of the South Sea Company and newly-elected member of parliament for Andover. His will indicates the vast wealth he accumulated in his comparatively short working life. At a conservative estimate he left £100,000. Among his assets were land, houses, shops, warehouses and factories in three counties, together with a small fleet of coastal cargo boats. This huge fortune was earned by unremitting hard work, the ability to see and to seize every business opening, the courage to take calculated risks. Above all, Sir Ambrose was a brilliant organiser with a sure grasp of detail. Nor was he afraid to delegate authority, first to his son John and then to under-managers. Yet he was not conceited. He told the schoolmaster he engaged for his employees' children to teach his pupils what life had taught him—that no one is too old to learn or too wise to be taught.

It was the acute shortage of charcoal for his furnaces in the south and the lure of the north-east coalfields that brought

Sir Ambrose and Lady Crowley

By courtesy of the Vicar of Mitcham Parish Church, Surrey.

Crowley to Sunderland, where he set up iron and steel works, manned largely by foreigners. Then he discovered that the water of the Derwent was peculiarly suited to the tempering of steel and coal supplies were more accessible so he moved the works and the unprotesting hands to Swalwell and Winlaton. There he recruited local labour, sent officials into the metal-working districts of Yorkshire and the Midlands to attract men to the North with the promise of paying their removal expenses and advertised in the *Post Bag*, offering steady employment to skilled workers who could make anything from a nail to an anchor. Sir Ambrose used only the best raw materials and imported bar-iron from Sweden, where he sent his half-brother for a year to investigate its manufacture. He solved the problem of eliminating the brittleness apparent in iron bars made in coal-fired furnaces[6] and initiated a new process. There seems to have been one department of the Crowley Works where visitors were not welcome.[7] It was here presumably that experiments were conducted from which evolved the production of shear steel, made by hammering together hot faggoted bars of blister steel and so ensuring evenness of content and texture. The exact date on which success was achieved is uncertain but manufacture was in full swing long before shear steel was available in Sheffield (1767).[8] Crowley's reputation as an ironmaster was such that William Penn, seeking assistance in the development of Pennsylvania, secured his personal directions for the working of iron and, through the years, the colony's output passed muster if it came up to Crowley's standards.

To store his merchandise Crowley had warehouses at Swalwell, Blaydon, Upper-Thames Street, London, and Greenwich, later the site of the Greenwich Power Station. Agents were in charge of these repositories and of the distribution of goods at home and abroad, hoes for the plantations in the West Indies, harpoons for the Greenland whale fisheries, nails, anchors and weapons for lucrative government contracts. No transaction was considered too paltry. Advertisements appeared in the *Newcastle Courant*, which attracted small, local customers from Bowes' agent at Gibside to a humble gardener at Winlaton. The Newcastle agent must have had an uneasy time for he never knew when Crowley would step ashore from one of the company's boats to reassure himself that neither at the works nor during transit was there any negligence or pilfering of goods, about which he held strong views, embodied in the Law Book of the Crowley Ironworks.[9] Be it noted, however, that Newcastle Common Council books prove that Crowley was not so particular about his payment of river tolls and for years he loaded and unloaded his ships without licence from the Corporation.

On Sir Ambrose's death the works passed to his son John,

then to the latter's widow, Mrs. Theodosia Crowley, who was more than a mere figurehead, although she took Isaac Millington into partnership. For over a century and a half the firm flourished under Crowley guidance. On their visits to England distinguished foreigners like Jars and, especially, Swedish engineers and metallurgists included the Crowley factories in their itinerary. Kalmeter speaks of their wealth and extent; Schröderstierna, responsible for the development of high-grade iron manufacture in Sweden, was impressed by the cast-iron cylindrical bellows used at Swalwell and by the anchors, hand-forged with sledge-hammers, which were reckoned the best in England. Indeed, it was not until 1790 that Crowleys lost their monopoly of naval work to the rival firm of Hawks of Gateshead. Angerstein, Director of Steel Works, toured Tyneside in 1753 and concentrated his enquiries on the Crowley factories. His interest was twofold. The increasing skill of English technologists presented a growing threat to the Swedish export trade and, whereas previously Sweden had provided half our imports of bar-iron, Russia was now in the market. Crowleys consumed 2,300 tons per annum, of which 2,000 were imported, so their custom was worth keeping.[10]

Millingtons purchased the works in 1783 and later sold out to Powe and Fawcus of North Shields. Eventually they were taken over by Raine and Co. Ltd., who moved to their present site at Derwenthaugh. If the secret of shear steel was carried from Crowleys to Sheffield, the wheel has turned full circle for Raine and Co. Ltd. are part of the Empire Rib Group.

Is it possible to reconcile the seemingly irreconcilable epithets of 'benevolent despot', 'semi-socialist', 'Mussolini', bestowed upon Sir Ambrose Crowley?

Hutchinson remarked that only after the works were functioning to his satisfaction did Sir Ambrose turn his attention to the institution of a code of rules, designed primarily for the owner's benefit and, as a secondary consideration, for the well-being of the employees. It is noteworthy that Crowley's commemorative monument in Mitcham

Parish Church observes the same order; from praise of his 'indefatigable industry and application to business' it proceeds to his 'true practice of Christianity and particularly a boundless liberality towards the poor.'

The formidable body of laws, each prefixed, in the founder's day, by three uncompromising words—'I do order'—was, under his son's direction, administered by a court of arbitration, meeting every ten weeks under the chairmanship of the chaplain, two representatives appointed by the management and two elected by the workmen, all of whom had the right of appeal to the court. Its efficiency is proved by its continued existence for over a century. The regulations provided, *inter alia*, for a system of stock-keeping 'to check carelessness in some clerks and knavery in others,' the locking-up every night of all materials, the daily inspection of cash and accounts, the prevention of the abuse of tools, a system of time-keeping based on an eighty-hour week, the training of foremen who, with tactful avoidance of fault-finding, were to make every man clearly understand his job. John Crowley saw to it that no local firm poached his well-drilled hands by an additional clause which required every workman to give six months' notice and a guarantee that he would not work within forty miles of Newcastle. The penalty for contravention of this rule was £50, which no one could afford.

The employees, who were expected to go to bed on the stroke of the nine o'clock curfew,[11] were housed in company property[12] or in leased houses for which the firm accepted responsibility. A doctor's services were provided and a workmen's compensation scheme inaugurated, whereby the sick could have an advance of wages and disabled or aged men received a weekly pension of five to seven shillings. Their widows got half-a-crown or a light job at the factory. While all biographers elaborate these benefits, only one[13] has seen fit to record that the recipients had to wear a badge inscribed 'Crowley's Poor' on their left shoulder.

Sir Ambrose, who considered good hand-writing essential for success in business, set up day schools to teach the work-

The end of the anchor shaft was forged ready to take the anchor arms. As many as ten heats would have been used to bring the bloom to this stage.

Stages in the forging of an eighteenth century anchor.
The production of complex shapes in iron could not be achieved with existing machinery. The operation became something in the nature of a piece of blacksmithing. Marine anchors, for example, were mainly forged by manual hammering.

The masterforger (Fig. 1) supervised closely the welding of the claw to the anchor arm, – his rule was used to indicate precisely where the hammer blows should fall. The team of four hammer men struck the red-hot workpiece in rapid succession while a fifth man (Fig. 2) steadied the iron on the anvil.

Joining the arm to the shaft required the rapid bringing together of the two parts at high temperature. Two hearths were used, the one on the right for the arm, and the other, in the background, for the shaft. Cranes carried the separate items, swinging them together over the anvil. Immediately the parts were in position the forger (Fig. 7) engaged the clutch to supply water to the wheel and knocked out the trip hammer support (Q). Then 'the most violent blows imaginable are struck as rapidly as possible . . . so that the arm is welded to the shaft in less time than it takes to read of it'.

After attaching a second arm, the chisel man (Fig. 1) knocked off burrs and finished off the anchor surface, working over a pit to allow the anchor to be worked from all four sides in succession.

Eighteenth century combined rolling and slitting mill.

After heating for at least one hour in the wood-burning oven, Y 1, the bar was then steadily reduced by progressively smaller gaps between the successive pairs of rolls (C, D, V, U, etc.). The bar illustrated emerges as rods having passed through the slitting mill. Power was provided by two water wheels, one of which can be seen on the extreme left.

men's children the three Rs and encouraged religious instruction by the foundation of a chapel, where daily services were held by a minister appointed by the firm. To provide his stipend and meet the upkeep of the building Crowley gave £10 a year and deducted a compulsory half-farthing in the shilling from the men's wages. Despite this arbitrary action Crowley was, judged by the standards of his age, surprisingly tolerant. Of Quaker stock, he joined the Church of England but fought vigorously for the religious freedom of his Roman Catholic employees, on whose behalf he petitioned the King. The latter promptly transferred all responsibility to the Bishop of Durham.

It is doubtful whether the Bishop's intervention had much effect on 'Crowley's Crew'. There were a boisterous crowd.

Under the old régime they were 'high Tory' and would have come to blows with any promoter of reform in church or state. The company rules were more often honoured in the breach than in the observance. The churchwardens' books of Ryton Parish Church show payments to the clerk and constable at Winlaton for enforcing the curfew and preserving the Sabbath calm. The only opponents to rout the 'Crew' were the keelmen of Newcastle and their wives. No pressgang ever conscripted a Crowley man. Armed with the tools of their trade and a grip like that of their heaviest anchors, the hands closed ranks and bore down upon the invaders who invariably fled in disorder. A perpetual state of war existed between the aggressive 'Crowley's Crew' and 'Hawks' Blacks' of Gateshead.[14] The Swalwell hoppings, where ironworkers and pitmen wrestled, ran races, grinned for tobacco and patronised Raw's, the local inn, were disrupted by running battles. The participants must have been an incongruous sight, pantalooned and cravatted, with blue, purple or yellow coats, or wearing second-hand buckskin breeches and cast-off jackets.[15] In Mrs. Theodosia Crowley's day the ironworkers became enthusiastic supporters of the Chartist movement and often constituted a serious threat to the peace. The fights with 'Hawks' Blacks', the occasional brushes with the Gibside and Chopwell gamekeepers were of little moment compared with their action in 1767 when they petitioned the Durham magistrates against the high price of farm produce and, failing to get legal assistance, ambushed the carts on their way to market and forced the farmers to sell at their price.

Sir Ambrose and his successors were evidently wise in keeping a tight hand on the employees, who appear to have borne them no ill-will. While we may query the claim that thousands daily praised Heaven for the Crowleys' virtues and wept when the last of the name died,[16] it is an indisputable fact that they had men with over fifty years' service, which is as good a testimonial as any employer could desire.

The Crowleys were well-situated for the transport of goods from their Tyneside works. As far as Blaydon the river was

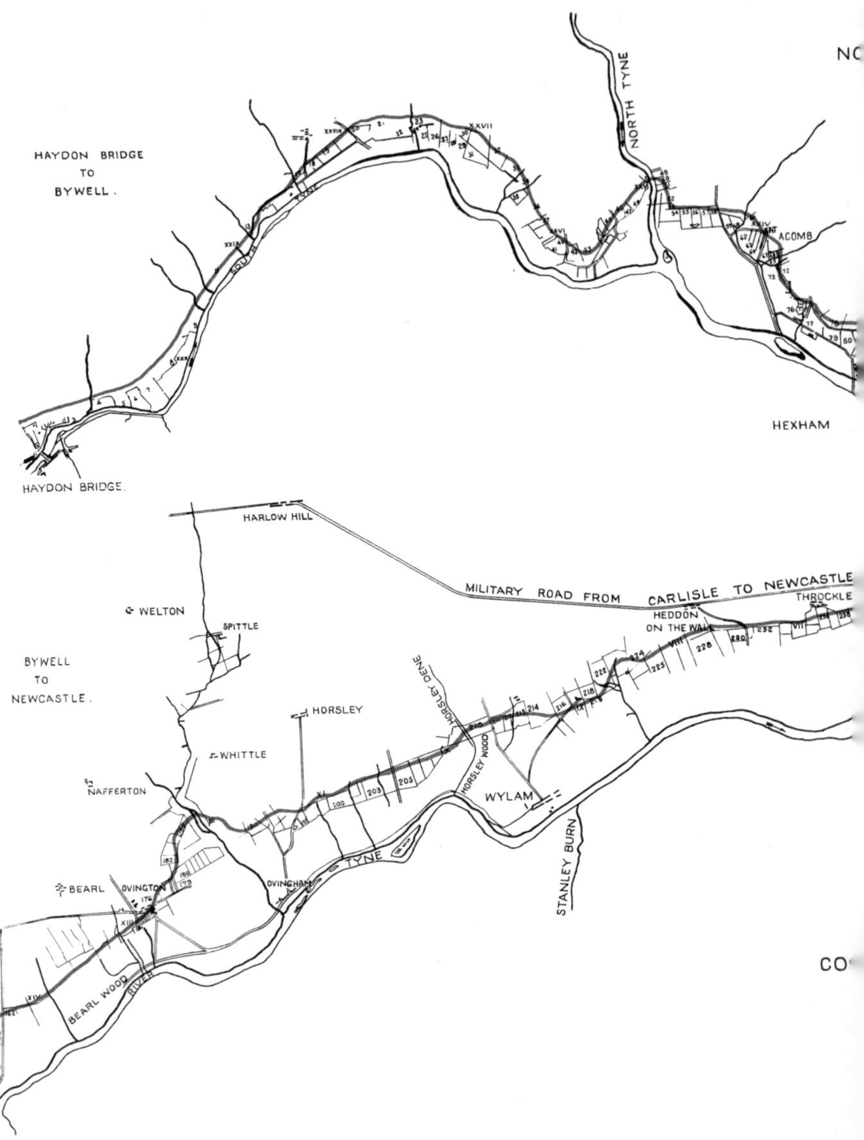
HAYDON BRIDGE
TO
BYWELL.
HAYDON BRIDGE.
NORTH TYNE
ACOMB
HEXHAM
HARLOW HILL
MILITARY ROAD FROM CARLISLE TO NEWCASTLE
THROCKLEY
HEDDON
ON THE WALL
WELTON
SPITTLE
BYWELL
TO
NEWCASTLE.
HORSLEY
WHITTLE
HORSLEY DENE
HORSLEY WOOD
NAFFERTON
WYLAM
STANLEY BURN
BEARL
OVINGTON
OVINGHAM
TYNE
RIVER
BEARL WOOD
BYWELL LANE

:RLAND.

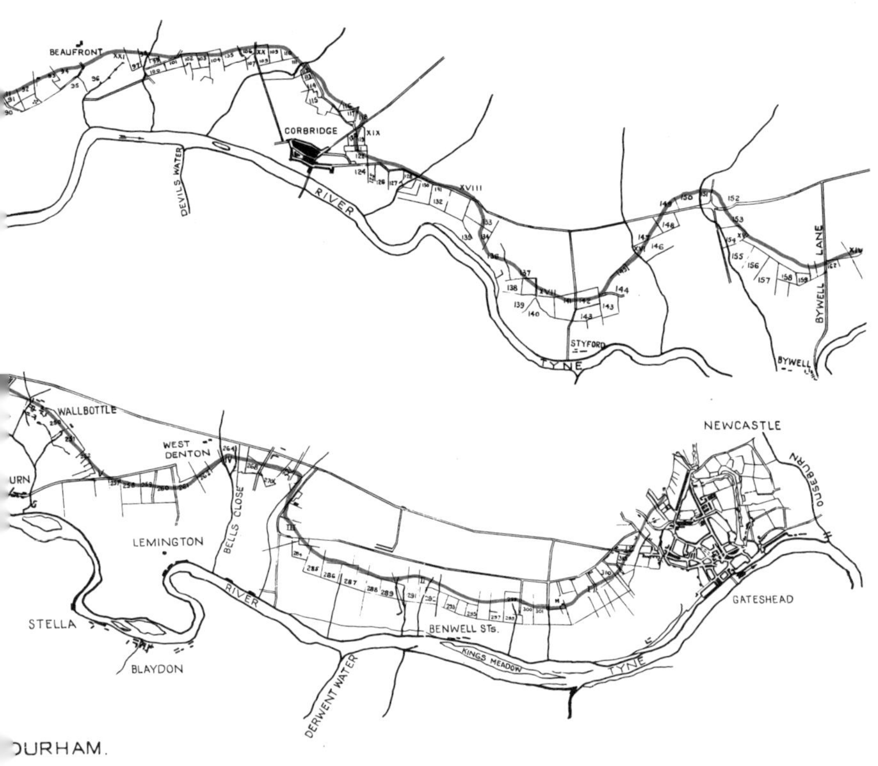

Plan of Canal from Chapman's Original

By courtesy of the Clerk to Peace of the County of Northumberland

navigable for keels whose loads were trans-shipped to the firm's cargo fleet. Smaller undertakings, trying to break into the national market, found themselves in difficulties. Long-distance road-haulage, involving the use of carts or pack-horses, was very expensive. Apart from the losses inflicted by highwaymen, the roads were in a parlous state. Modern road-making is the concern of the Ministry of Transport and the tax-payers, and the cost of one rural mile of dual carriageway can be £1,000,000. In the eighteenth century, road maintenance was the responsibility of the parish, no matter how poverty-striken, through which it ran. Hence repairs were delayed until the situation was wellnigh irremediable. Road engineering did not properly begin until the last quarter of the century. The passage of mail coaches was thereby expedited but the cost of conveyance of goods remained high. Water-borne trade was quicker and cheaper so, from 1721 onwards, rivers were dredged and deepened, not without protest from horse breeders and dealers who feared a loss of livelihood. The improving of rivers opened up the way for canals which, in turn, came in for unfounded criticism from farmers, road-menders and those engaged in river and coastal trade. Nevertheless, before the end of the century, hundreds of miles of canals were in use and hundreds more in the planning stage. Speculative canal promotion was at its height in 1792–93 when some thirty schemes were afoot but the impetus had slackened by 1797. Acknowledgment and profits went to the shareholders, not to the engineer, highly competent though he might be. He was not only a consultant; he was responsible for costing, for negotiating land purchase and compensating owners, for hiring and directing the labour force, for the supply of materials. James Watt received £80, which included travelling and boarding expenses, for a seven-weeks' survey of the Perth-Coupar terrain, when he worked a twelve-hour day, and his charge of seven guineas for the design of a new bridge over the Clyde at Hamilton was accepted in preference to that of Smeaton who had the audacity to ask £10.

Northumberland remained one of the few counties without

a canal until, in 1794, William Chapman (1750–1832) was appointed consulting engineer to the promoters of an east-west canal from Newcastle to Maryport.

He was the son of a shrewd Whitby sea captain trading between the Baltic and the Tyne who later settled in Saville Row, Newcastle, and established a ropery at Willington. The elder Chapman was more than a first class mariner; he was something of a scientist. On one occasion he landed at Shields with his latest discovery, desalinated sea water. His friends at the Lawe and the Low Lights risked testing it in the form of punch which they pronounced excellent, while the *Transactions of the Royal Society* (1758) published his findings. As often happened in those days, Chapman's idea was pirated and he received no financial benefit from the process which had great potentialities in the days of long voyages under sail, when the shortage of fresh water was an ever-present danger. One wonders how he would have reacted to contemporary developments in this field of research which engage the attention of our Water Resources Board and Atomic Engery Authority in conjunction with Weir Westgarth, Ltd.[17]

His son had every prospect of a successful career in the merchant service. He was in command of his ship at the age of eighteen but he was more interested in harbour installations than in navigation and he decided to become a civil engineer. He was encouraged in this new venture by two older men of wide experience, Watt and Boulton, the former an earnest, diffident inventor, akin to Chapman in temperament and interests, the latter an enterprising business man and an unerring judge of character.

Chapman first came to the fore as resident engineer for the County of Kildare canal, part of the Grand Canal on which he later worked. While in Kildare he improved upon the existing type of skew bridge, considered dangerous to travellers, particularly at night. The joints of the voussoirs, whether of brick or stone, were set at right angles to the face of the oblique arch instead of parallel with the abutments, so ensuring that the canal bridge suited the line of the road. One such

William Chapman (1750–1832)
By courtesy of the Director, Science Museum, South Kensington

bridge was successfully built but, apart from airing his views in an article,[18] Chapman did not pursue the idea. He lacked skilled overseers and good material; the execution was costly and he felt there was need for further research. Charles Hutton, in his standard work, *The Principles of Bridges* (1772), makes no mention of this development, although he must have been aware of it. Chapman's next assignment was the reconstruction of a five-span bridge over the Liffey, where he encountered and overcame the difficulties caused by quicksand under one of the piers. His work in Ireland earned for him membership of the Royal Irish Academy and a spate of offers of professional engagements in Great Britain.

The first he accepted was that of surveying a line for a canal from the North Sea to the Solway. He made two surveys and wrote detailed reports (1795–1797), logically set out in straightforward language, to vindicate his own findings and answer his chief rivals, Dodd and Sutcliffe.

There was no disagreement over the advantages of such a waterway. Small towns and villages would benefit from an easier outlet for their products, slate from Shap, gloves and felt hats from Hexham, limestone from Corbridge, and the country folk could bring their garden produce into Newcastle market for a two-shilling return fare. Newcastle would become a second Birmingham by attracting new factories and extending her boundaries with a consequent increase in land values. Her already considerable export trade would be increased by ready access to inland towns, while a seller's market awaited development in Ireland. The speeding-up of the transit of goods would make for a quicker turnover and the safe passage of cargoes through the canal and the Irish Sea would reduce insurance rates in time of war.[19] A discreet silence was maintained over the advice to exporters on New Year's Day, 1794, of another rise in freight charges to meet the demands of seamen and dockers for higher wages.

In plotting the course of the canal Chapman avoided the tidal waters of the Tyne on the grounds that the river was too wide and prone to flooding, when the gravel and stones it brought down formed massive shoals, aggravated by the indiscriminate dumping of ballast. Canal boats were not fit craft for such a tideway. He favoured the north side of the river and, after a re-assessment of his original survey, advocated a canal which would skirt north Newcastle and run via Elswick, Horsley, Corbridge, Beaufront, Hexham, St. John Lee, Warden to Haydon Bridge, a distance of 30.75 miles at an estimate cost of £3,737 per mile. This section was to be constructed first, with collaterals opening up the country to the north. The second stage would have been the extension to Maryport via Bardon Mill, Haltwhistle, Brampton, Carlisle, Wigton and Allonby, with collaterals to Penrith.

Chapman's plan was inspected by Jessop and Whitworth who considered the project would amply repay the shareholders, praised his careful work, impartiality and cautious costing, and pronounced the line the best of those put forward. They added a warning that some areas, especially Whittle Dene and St. John Lee, presented grave engineering problems which would necessitate local deviations as excavation progressed. From previous experience Chapman was fully aware of such contingencies and he was always open to reasoned argument. His rivals abandoned reason for the sorriest form of criticism—personal recrimination. Dodd, a competent engineer, was resentful because he considered himself the originator of the scheme and had already worked out a line along the south bank of the river with the support—so he claimed—of every landowner concerned, which would eliminate expensive aqueducts, tunnels and bridges, open up wider markets, earn greater profits for the investors and arouse less opposition than any other Canal Navigation Bill before Parliament. In Dodd's view Chapman was guilty of gross and lavish absurdity, of furthering his private interests, incompetent and lamentably slow, the result of inhaling too much Irish air. Dodd's witticisms stung Chapman, in the course of an otherwise restrained and business-like evaluation of the merits and de-merits of the two courses, to one sharp rejoinder. He found it inexcusable 'that any person styling himself a *Civil Engineer* should *be thus grossly ignorant of the rudiments of that profession*.'

The unsuccessful Sutcliffe, whose strictures were courteously refuted by Chapman, was like a persistent mosquito buzzing round an elephant. Sutcliffe approved neither of Chapman's plan nor of Dodd's. He knew a good line could be found along the south bank. He had found it. The north side was impossible. It would ruin private estates, the cost was

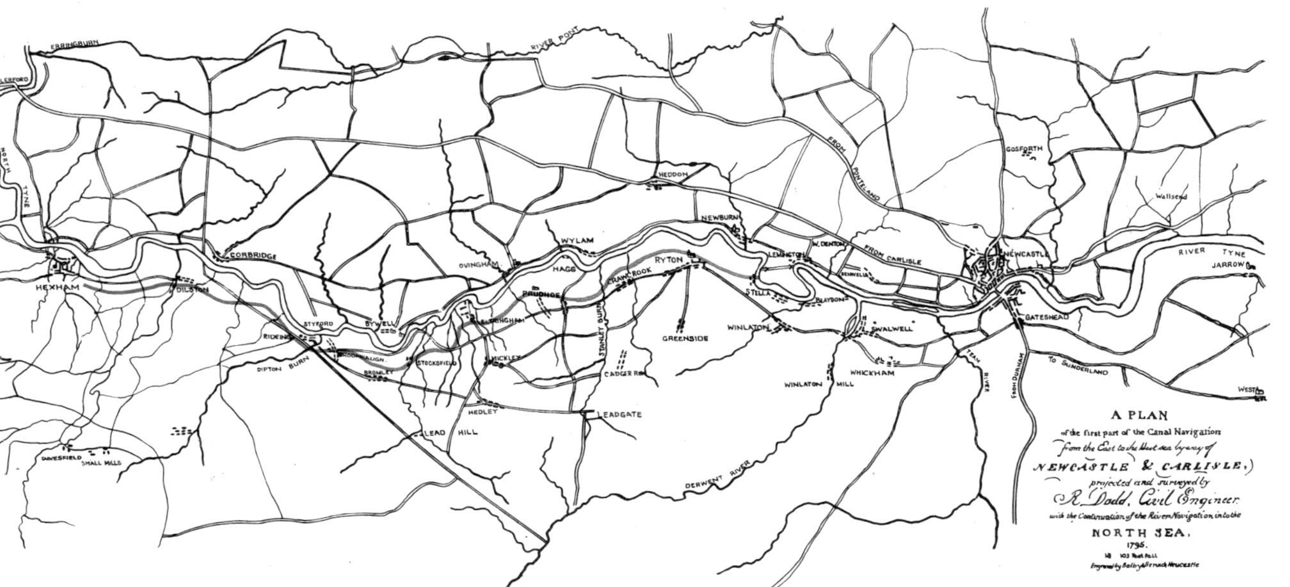

Dodd's Proposed Canal for the South side of the River Tyne

substantially underestimated, the surveyor was inexperienced,[20] the projected reservoirs were 'fitter for duck ponds than auxiliaries for a canal', a remark that scarcely equated with his statement that they would deluge his Grace the Duke of Northumberland's collieries. Sutcliffe even inferred that a canal on the north side would freeze over in winter, whereas one on the south, if built by him and not by Dodd, would always have free water. His long reports are confused, full of trivialities and the weaknesses which he blindly attributed to his rivals. He had to undergo a gruelling six-day cross-examination when the Bill came before the Parliamentary Committee (1797) and was forced to admit, in his own words, that he had 'never finished no canal'. The official finding on his testimony was that his imagination was equal to the task of supplying all the data of which he was professionally ignorant.

Lack of adequate local support forced the promoters to withdraw the Bill. Tyneside was not canal-minded.[21] Four landowners, Bewicke, Errington, Hodgson and Hunter, petitioned against the Bill, as did the incumbent of St. John Lee, his churchwarden and eighty villagers. The strongest supporters were the Commissioners and Governors of the Royal Hospital for Seamen, Greenwich, which owned huge estates along the projected line. North Shields' petition on behalf of the canal contained 85 names, Morpeth's 136 and Newcastle, out of a population of 25,000, could muster only 258 supporters.

Dodd's scheme never reached Parliament but Chapman had some compensation for his years of wasted work in the following century. It was then that he devoted most of his time to mining and steam locomotion and was appointed engineer to the promoters of the Newcastle and Carlisle Railway. Nor did his reputation as a civil engineer suffer. When he was seventy-eight his services were still in demand. He collaborated with Rennie on the London Dock and the South Dock and Basin at Hull; he was engineer for Scarborough, Seaham and Leith harbours, for which he was recommended by the First

Lord of the Admiralty; he was consultant for bridges and approach roads at North Shields and Scotswood.

Private concerns, in which he was co-partner with his brother Edward, also claimed his attention. He developed the rope works at Willington, originally established by his father, patented (1797—1798) *La Valseuse*, a machine for producing a rope of indeterminate length, and a new method of twisting cordage which superseded the old way of making shroud-laid rope. Chapman claimed that the process was applicable to the manufacture of any type of rope and of worsted or cotton yarn. Robert Hood Haggie acquired the ropery about 1840. Speaking at the firm's annual meeting in Newcastle upon Tyne in 1920, Stevenson Haggie, Chairman of the Company, recalled the water-colour[22] of the old works, set in a little Arcadia, with the Rose Inn on Rosehill Bank, then the summer residence of the mayor and aldermen of Newcastle. He remarked that *La Valseuse* was still used for a certain class of rope, thus proving that Chapman used good materials and well-designed machinery. A further proof of Chapman's efficiency was the fact that he made many of the great hempen cables for George III's navy, some of which were probably supplied to Nelson's fleet at Trafalgar. The *Royal George's* cable, 24 inches in circumference, made of tarred Russian hemp, lay under water in the sunken ship for sixty years. When raised the rope was perfectly fresh in the interior and a section preserved at the works was in good condition in 1920. Chapman's water system was also working at that date but the Watts Beam Condensing Engine, which he erected about 1789, was destroyed in the great fire of 1873.

Chapman seems to have been too diffident to enjoy much social life, too modest to assert himself. A man of temperate habits and wide interests, he was deeply attached to his immediate family, his 'beloved and faithful wife', his daughter, an only child, his brother Edward and sister Hannah, His will, which was proved at £8,000, shows his true concern and meticulous provision for their welfare after his death.

James Losh, Chairman of the Directors of the Newcastle

Willington Dene Viaduct, showing the old ropery.
From the watercolour by T. M. Richardson Senior

By courtesy of the Director and Curator, Laing Art Gallery, Newcastle upon Tyne

and Carlisle railway, commented that 'our engineer, William Chapman (though I believe well acquainted with his profession), is by no means an effective person.' In the capacity of Vice-President of the local Literary and Philosophical Society, he criticised as ill-planned and unconvincing, Chapman's lecture (later published) on the preservation of timber from decay. It is small wonder that Chapman took refuge in the written word, either as a reader in his private library[23] at his well-appointed home in Ridley Place, or as the writer of pamphlets on civil and mining engineering, the role of the workman in industry and politics, parliamentary reform, the attitude and duties of the Established Church, the state of agriculture and the effects of the Corn Laws.

His most appreciative obituary appeared in the *Caledonian Mercury* which stressed the benefits that his vast experience had conferred upon the shipping interests of the kingdom. The *Tyne Mercury*, *Newcastle Chronicle* and *Newcastle Courant* were content to reprint excerpts from the Scottish paper and to add a perfunctory 'In Newcastle he was universally respected and his death is most sincerely regretted.'

NOTES

1. *Blackwood's Magazine*, 3 September 1822.
2. Battie, *Treatise on Madness* (1758); Pargeter, *Observations on Maniac Disorders* (1792); Pinel, *Traité Médico-Philosophique sur l'Aliénation Mentale* (1809).
3. Moxon, *Mechanick Exercises* (1683); Harris, *Lexicon Technicum* (1704); Gautier, *Traité des Ponts* (1716); Belidor, *Science des Ingénieurs* (1729).
4. He has been identified with the Jack Anvil of *The Spectator,* No. 299, 12 February 1712, whose wife made him change his name to the more elegant Sir John Enville. Sir Ambrose was connected by marriage with Sir William Stanhope, brother of the Earl of Chesterfield.
5. *Vide:* W. A. Young, *Works Organisation in the Eighteenth Century; Transactions of the Newcomen Society*, 1924; M. W. Flinn, *Industry and Technology in the Derwent Valley*, *ibid.* 1955; *Men of Iron*, 1962.
6. G. Jars, *Voyages Métallurgiques,* 1774–1781.
7. W. Hutchinson, *History and Antiquities of the County Palatine of Durham* (Vol. II), 1785.
8. It has been suggested that the process was taken to Sheffield by a man called Eltringham. A possible explanation is that Laidler of London, who established an unsuccessful factory at Eltringham, which was to have become a 'little Birmingham', and who disappeared somewhat

hastily, was in fact responsible. *Vide* T. Bewick, *Memoir of Thomas Bewick, Written by Himself*, 1822–1828.

9. The MSS. of 307 folios offers a unique source of material for students of economic and social history.
10. 10 per cent. of the total imports into England.
11. The original curfew bell is at the Delta Works of Raine & Co. Ltd.
12. The weekly rent ranged from 5¼d. to 6½d.
13. W. Bourn, *History of the Parish of Ryton*, 1896.
14. Their leader was Ned White, whose partner at local dances was Nanny the Mazer. Her exploits are still recounted in North Country broadcasts.
15. John Selkirk's contemporary Tyneside song, *Swalwell Hoppings*.
16. W. Hutchinson, *op. cit.*
17. The first international conference on desalination was held in Washington, October 1965. Britain's delegation was led by Professor R. S. Silver, co-inventor of the cheapest known method of large-scale desalination. Weir Westgarth have built over half the plant now operating throughout the world, including that at Kuwait, which produces 6,000,000 gallons of fresh water daily.
18. *Oblique Arches*, *Rees Cyclopedia* (Vol. XXV), London, 1819.
19. With a brief interval during the uneasy Peace of Amiens we were at war with France 1793–1815.
20. He admitted that he had never met Chapman and knew nothing about him.
21. This attitude appears to be unchanged. It was pointed out in 1943 that a local canal would have given employment to 8,000 men and saved an enormous tonnage of coastal shipping in World War II. More recently (1965), the plan, published by the Inland Waterways Association, of a £300,000,000 Grand Contour Canal to link Tyne and Tees with Southampton had a very cool reception.
22. By the local artist, T. M. Richardson, senior.
23. Light reading was at a discount. He had only one novel among 535 books.

4
GOLDSMITHS

A growing interest, both at home and abroad, in the collection of antique English silver had been matched by a steep increase in price.[1] The original makers would be dumbfounded if they could compare the prices they received with those prevailing today. In 1967, for example, the gold[2] Freedom Box presented by the Master and Brethren of Trinity House, Newcastle, to Admiral Keppel on his acquittal after court-martial[3] changed hands at Christie's for £2,205. It was made by a local goldsmith, John Langlands, for £74, 15s. od.[4] A silver tankard by the same maker fetched £520 at Phillips, Son and Neale's in 1968. Reid and Sons of Newcastle have a receipt for a similar tankard, bought by Prince William of Gloucester in 1798 on on of his many visits to the town. The price? £10, 14s. od.[5] Langlands was a highly successful business man but such sums would have been beyond his comprehension.

Local goldsmiths, first mentioned in 1229, were twenty years later appointed assayers, 'fit and prudent', of the moneys for the King's mint. In 1423 the town received the rare privilege of having its own touch, a just cause for pride among the fraternity, but in the 1701 reorganization of Assay Offices, Newcastle was passed over. An indignant protest was drawn up, recalling ancient rights and stressing the hardships in store for Newcastle tradesmen if local silverware had to be sent to London for assay. Officialdom relented and the Newcastle Assay Office opened in 1702 with Francis Batty as the first Master.[6] A treasured possession of the Newcastle Company of Goldsmiths is the circular copper plate bearing the punches

Tankard 1754. Langlands and Goodrick

By courtesy of the Director and Curator, Laing Art Gallery, Newcastle upon Tyne

of the makers who assayed at Newcastle from that period. There are two hundred and eighty-seven different marks, most of them identifiable.

The best-known of our Assay Masters was the jovial Matthew Prior,[7] mathematical and musical intrument-maker, Bewick's friend and a favourite with the gentry of Northumberland and Durham, who appreciated his skill as an angler and sportsman. In his official capacity he displayed all the competence and determination of a true-born Tynesider. In 1773 the London Company, jealous of provincial rights of assay, insinuated that the country offices were guilty of gross irregularities, if not of downright fraud. Newcastle Corporation was up in arms and besought their Members of Parliament to protect the town's interests. Sir Walter Blackett was, alas, laid low with gout, but Matthew Ridley supported

Prior at a Committee of the House of Lords (22 March). On the same day he wrote to Langlands: '. . . he (Prior) acquitted himself with great precision and judgment, and the Committee came to a solution, That the Assay Office at Newcastle upon Tyne had been conducted with Fidelity and Skill . . .'. The Newcastle Company was so delighted with the decision that they paid Prior's expenses[8] and added a richly deserved bonus of five guineas. Prior had been no whit abashed by the august court of enquiry. When questioned about the accuracy of his scales, he declared that one hair from his hand would tilt the balance either way. As to his weights, which he promptly produced, they were true to within half a pennyweight—and London-made. His method of assay conformed to regulations and he took strong exception to any imputation that he was incompetent to judge the standard of the plate which came his way. Finally he made it abundantly clear that his fee of one halfpenny an ounce for the plate he assayed was far from exorbitant. The London Company admitted defeat and troubled Master Prior no more.

In 1536 the goldsmiths had been incorporated with the plumbers, glaziers, pewterers and painters who, from 1619, met in the Morden Tower to the restoration of which the goldsmiths subscribed a quarter of the members' contributions. Their association terminated in 1717 when a difference of opinion with the glaziers forced them to seek new quarters. Up Painter Heugh and across Dean Court they went, to Assayer's Hall[9] where, for an annual rental of £1, they met as an independent body.

They were a closely knit community and mutually helpful. The Bulmans were among those who had caused to be grateful to them. In 1730 an apprentice, Robert Aynsley, ran off with some of their stock but was tracked down by the Company who dealt summarily with thief and receiver. Thirteen years later George Bulman died at the age of forty and his widow was left with six young children. She struggled in vain to carry on the business. Within eighteen months a meeting of creditors was called. The stock-in-trade and tools were quickly disposed of, but the house and shop were still unsold in 1747 and a number of customers had failed to settle their accounts. Meanwhile the condition of the hapless Ann Bulman, consigned to Newgate until such time as she could discharge her liabilities, was relieved by a grant from the Newcastle goldsmiths. It is pleasing to be able to record that she survived her ordeal and lived to a ripe old age.

As employers the goldsmiths were equally considerate, as we learn from several references to the length of service—in some cases fifty years—of their workmen. Such a one was Thomas Blackett, Langlands' foreman and godfather of Bewick, who tells us[10] how highly Langlands valued Blackett's honesty and punctuality and how often he quietly slipped half a guinea into the hand of ex-employees who were too old or infirm to work.

The goldsmiths were also outward-looking and readily identified themselves with the general welfare of Newcastle. Individually and collectively they contributed to the upkeep of the Infirmary, the Dispensary and the four charity schools of the town. In 1771 Matthew Prior evolved a novel fund-raising scheme. An enormous 'plate of parting', weighing 8,005 oz. 15 dwts., reputedly the largest ever tested in Britain and valued at £3,702, 13s. 4½d., came from Cox's refinery at Bill Quay to Prior's workshop in the Side. He exhibited the plate at a shilling a head to curious sightseers and the Infirmary was the richer by eight guineas.

Some members of the Company took an active part in civic life. The modest role of serjeant-at-mace was at one time filled by Thomas Gill; that of sword-bearer to the Corporation by Robert Makepeace and Robert Pinkney. William Ramsay was mayor in 1701, while the energetic John Langlands was coroner, common-councillor, commissioner for the 1763 street-lighting scheme and trustee for the building of the temporary and new bridges after the floods of 1771. Yet the services of a Ramsay or a Langlands brought no social advancement to the goldsmiths as a whole. They remained superior craftsmen and tradesmen for the élite of the dealers in precious metals were always the bankers.

It is therefore somewhat surprising that more than one hundred and fifty local eighteenth-century goldsmiths and apprentices have been traced. Sons of clergymen, yeomen and nurserymen, bricklayers and bakers, cheesemongers and cordwainers, master mariners and maltmakers, smiths and skinners, they flocked in from Cumberland, Northumberland and Yorkshire to serve an apprenticeship of seven to ten years[11] which cost their guardians from £12, 12s. 0d. to £40 in premiums. It was an exacting course, at first spent on repetitive processes, then on concentrated attention to minute and intricate detail, which called for a highly developed artistic sense. Leisure time was brief and its use circumscribed by strict regulations.

Hence only a small percentage of these aspirants made their mark. The course was too long and arduous for George Dixon, son of a Cumbrian millwright and apprenticed to Langlands. He deserted his master's service after four years. Robert Aynsley and his boon companion, Luke Killingworth Potts, put themselves beyond the pale by embezzling their respective masters' property. Richard Hobbs, maker of the famous Morpeth monteith (1712), retired into obscurity six years later. Some, lacking the necessary capital or business acumen, were content to be trustworthy journeymen and foremen. Among them were John Goresuch, who worked for Cookson, Thomas Blackett and James McClymond, employed by Langlands for over half a century. The lure of wider horizons claimed not a few, of whom the most adventurous was Hesilrigg Metcalf, the only surviving son of a Newcastle tinman. He emigrated to Jamaica where he died about 1760. Then, as now, London was the Mecca of inexperienced youth. Regardless of the fact that London had more than sufficient native goldsmiths and that it was full of pitfalls for the unwary provincial, three of our worthies, George Chalmers, Robert Makepeace and Timothy Williamson, made their way there. Makepeace went into business in Searle Street, near Lincoln's Inn, and Chalmers could afford the time and money to travel to Newcastle to vote in the elections of 1777 and 1780. Perhaps he regaled his old companions with tales of life in the great capital, a life which swallowed up poor Williamson without leaving a trace behind. Less venturesome than Williamson but eminently successful was Stephen Buckle who returned to work in his native York, whence he reappeared to vote at the burgesses' elections of 1741. He was also admitted free of York by patrimony and became a Chamberlain of that city, 1748–49.[12]

The traffic of goldsmiths between Newcastle and London seems to have been a one-way affair. Only one instance[13] has been traced of a London firm—Sharp and Williams of The Strand—venturing to send a representative here with sample wares, while working foreign goldsmiths were cold-shouldered, as John Huet discovered early in the century. His claim to kinship with Dr. Huet, Bishop of Avranches, did not impress the local Company who fined a fellow-member, Jonathan French, £5 because he had dealt with this foreigner who worked in Gateshead. The outcome of the affair was a decision (12 August 1724) that no goldsmith accepted free of Newcastle was to work with or for any person within a seven-mile radius who was not free of the town.[14] Among the ten signatories to this minute was a presumably repentant Jonathan French. Huet clearly thrived on opposition and was not embittered by the action of his Newcastle rivals. At his death in 1738 he left a sizable estate out of which he made handsome bequests to local charities.

Of the goldsmiths working in Newcastle many were men in a small way of business who, on an average, assayed two hundred ounces of silver per annum and confined themselves to making rings, buttons, buckles and spoons. Yet goldsmiths of substance and reputation emerged in each quarter of the century. Experts differ as to their comparative importance and comparisons are proverbially odious but Isaac Cookson, John Langlands and Christian Ker Reid made noteworthy contributions to the age in which they lived. Examples of their work are on view in the Laing Art Gallery and at the Civic Centre, Newcastle upon Tyne.

So wide was the variety of silverware in demand in the eighteenth century that many London goldsmiths began to specialize but the leading Newcastle craftsmen, dealing with a more restricted clientèle, seem to have preferred to build up a general stock. Raw material was in short supply at the beginning of the period. Exports far exceeded imports for the East India Company, in 1717, shipped abroad 3,000,000 ounces of silver and there was also a brisk clandestine trade with the Continent. Although silver from the Alston Moor lead mines was refined locally by the Ryton Company, the London Lead Company and the Blackett family, these firms dealt direct with London. The sight of the ore being loaded at Newcastle quay must have riled potential local buyers, especially as the London Lead Company were reputed to be the best refiners in the country.

However, they could buy on the open market at an average price of 5s. 8d. per ounce. They also bought and melted down debased coinage and outmoded goods. There were other sources of supply, some bordering on the illegitimate and occasionally overstepping the bounds. From time to time treasure trove, in which the North was particularly rich, found its way to the goldsmiths' workshops. There are frequent references in old records to the discovery in Northumberland and Durham of Roman coins and articles of vertu turned up by ploughmen, ditchers and road-menders. Whether such finds came into the hands of the Newcastle goldsmiths depended on the vigilance of the lord of the manor or his agent. Isaac Cookson was to find himself in a predicament over this source of supply. Goldsmiths had no foolproof means of distinguishing between stolen goods and second-hand articles offered for sale by the genuine owners. They had to rely upon a sixth and fallible sense, their intuition. Langlands exercised his intuition to some purpose when in 1761 he handed over to the authorities a 'Captain Thomas Watson of the Royal Volunteers', who tried to sell him some silver spoons. The bogus captain, who was in fact a Shilbottle collier, was committed to Newgate as a common thief.

It is naturally impossible to discover whether any local men availed themselves of what were known in thieves' *argot* as 'white soup' (stolen silver, metled down) and 'brown gravy' (gold). Such transactions were never disclosed.

Church silver had been sadly depleted by Puritanical iconoclasts in the time of Edward VI and by the crusade against Popery at the beginning of Elizabeth's reign. Flagons, chalices, patens, candlesticks and alms dishes were urgently required in innumerable town and country churches throughout the northern counties. The need was met by local goldsmiths, notably Cookson and Langlands, and much of their work is extant today.

It was often commissioned by parishioners. In 1722 Robert Rymer left to St. John's Church, Newcastle, a large flagon, chalice and paten, the work of Francis Batty, junior, valued in his day at £60. The earliest piece of church plate bearing the mark of Isaac Cookson (1729) became the property of Warden Church. John Huet, the ostracized foreigner, presented a paten to his Parish Church of Whickham in 1731. Blyth received in 1762 a cup and paten made by Langlands. Both were elaborately inscribed with the arms of White Ridley and bore the motto *Constans Fidei*. Seven years later the same firm accepted an unusual assignment, a flagon made in accordance with the terms of the will of Richard Walker, yeoman of Harton, who desired that 'his silver tankard and gill be made into a flaggon and delivered to Jarrow Church, for the use of the communion table.' The set of four alms dishes by Langlands and Robertson and the christening basin by Pinkey and Scott, which belonged to All Saints' Church, are now in the Laing Art Gallery.

In such ways the depredations of earlier years were made good.

In the domestic sphere the possibilities were endless, ranging from dredgers to dinner plates, from cake-baskets to coffee-pots, from tankards to tea equipages, whose style developed from the unadorned simplicity of Queen Anne's

Christening Bowl 1788. Pinkney and Scott
By courtesy of the Director and Curator of the Laing Art Gallery, Newcastle upon Tyne

day through the rococo period to the classical silverware of 1770–1800, thereby progressively testing the silversmith's skill in flat-hammering, chasing, embossing, engraving and piercing.

Tankards were always in great demand in Newcastle for the local beer of which Cunningham so heartily approved, while the outbreak of the Seven Years' War gave a nationwide impetus to beer-drinking. The previous heavy duty on gin had been removed but gin came from France and was therefore an unpatriotic drink. A popular song of the times upheld with raucous vigour 'The profits and pleasures of stout British beer' and proclaimed that beer-drinking Britons could never be beat. An early tankard, in use about 1710–1720, had a handle fashioned into a whistle for the convenient summoning of the potman. Another variety, peculiar to York, Hull and Newcastle was of Danish origin. It was made as late as 1774 and had a row of pegs fitted inside to mark the diminishing level so that, in communal use, no one got more than his fair share.[15]

In some quarters tea-drinking was considered a vice, one which was difficult to eradicate. In his journal (May 1746) John Wesley lamented the addiction of the poor of Newcastle to their dish of tea on the score of the expense incurred, the injury done to the drinkers' health and the waste of time involved, but he ruefully admitted that he himself found it hard to break a twenty-six-year-old habit. Tea was certainly costly, hence the small size of early tea-pots and the appearance of the tea-kettle for frequent replenishment. In 1754 Edward and Willoughby Gibson at the Sign of the Canister in the Flesh Market advertised seventeen blends of tea from bohea at 5s. per pound to the finest hyson at 18s. The latter was, in all probability, coloured by locally manufactured copperas exported to the Far East and reimported in this somewhat different form. It was of course possible, but risky, to halve the price by dealing with a local smuggler.

The gentry willingly paid large sums for their tea equipages. John Thomlinson, the gay young curate of Rothbury, recalled that his aunt, the Rector's wife, pleaded for £50 to refurnish her drawing-room. She had ear-marked £20 for a silver tea-kettle, lamp and table. The dish of tea was often a preliminary to a convivial evening at the card-table. So anxious were some of our north-country hostesses to avoid any waste of this precious commodity that they spread the used tea-leaves on buttered bread and handed it round instead of cakes. It is rumoured that, at this stage of the festivities, the gentlemen hastily withdrew for a glass of wine.

My lady's toilet was also indebted to the goldsmith's art. Women's fashions—and men's too—changed rapidly through the century, becoming more and more bizarre. As a satirical rhymester said of the former, and might with equal truth have said of the latter:

> *Like the clock on the tower, that shows you the weather,*
> *You are hardly the same for two days together.*

The dainty arrangement of ribbons and laces, the careful

balance of monstrous hair styles called for the use of silver-framed mirrors, sconces, candlesticks and snuffers, which became as ornate as the prevailing taste in dress. Later candlesticks were fitted with ingenious devices to prevent specks of charred wick from settling on delicate fabrics. A silver tray held boxes for perfumes and pomades, while the wash-hand-stand had its complement of silver ewer and basin.

The master of the house shared the utilitarian articles but his alone was the sporting equipment of the day. Cock-fighting was popular throughout the period and the birds were armed with 'fair, round-pointed silver spurs.' The gentleman rider required silver bits, stirrups and spurs. If he was out with the hounds, he drank from a silver stirrup-cup which, in the last quarter of the century, was fashioned into the shape of a fox's head. Archery became increasingly popular in the north and competitors shot for gold and silver medals, quivers, gorgets, arrows and bugles. Nor was there any dearth of gold and silver cups, worth twenty-five to a hundred guineas, for the horse races.

Presentation plate was, with one known exception, a male prerogative and many pieces were commissioned to honour the public figures of the day. For their part in quelling the Newcastle corn riot of 1740, the Corporation voted a gold Freedom Box to Captain Sowle and silver salvers to Captain Fielding and Ensign Hewitt. On his return from Culloden the Duke of Cumberland received the freedom of Newcastle in a gold box. In fact the Duke did rather well for the Master and Brethren of Trinity House, Newcastle, made him a like presentation. Their box, of 'curious workmanship', was probably local work as they usually employed Newcastle firms, although only a brief note is extant, showing an expenditure of £4 for inscribing and decorating. In 1757 our politically-minded Common-Council voted gold Freedom Boxes to William Pitt, father of the famous Prime Minister, and to Henry Bilson Legge for their loyal disinterested services to king and country. Occasionally such honours came nearer home. On 23 September 1782 it was unanimously resolved that the Mayor, Edward Mosley[16] be thanked for his 'extraordinary attention and his great care, assiduity and trouble' in keeping the accounts for the rebuilding and completion of Tyne Bridge. The recognition took the form of a piece of gold plate, presented by Sir Matthew White Ridley.

Newcastle goldsmiths could and did meet all these demands. If their wares lacked the cachet of London goods, they were as carefully made and considerably cheaper. The abbé Le Blanc, by no means an out-and-out Anglophile, commented very favourably upon the solidity, neatness and striving after perfection which characterized the work of the provincial craftsman. He was less than just in saying that precision, akin to stiffness, was the Englishman's criterion of beauty.[17] Isaac Cookson's output disproved that thesis.

Cookson, a native of Penrith, was apprenticed for seven years to Francis Batty, junior, for a premium of £35. He was admitted free in 1728, set up in business in the middle of the Side and became the leading Newcastle goldsmith of the period. In the same year he had the honour of being elected warden and steward, a position which he held at frequent intervals throughout his career. In 1734 he voted at the Newcastle parliamentary elections.

An exhibition of local silver plate held in the Black Gate Museum (19–21 May 1897), displayed the wide range of Cookson's workmanship. Examples of his communion cups, flagons, patens and alms dishes, dating from 1729 to 1752, were lent by the officials of churches from Hartburn to Berwick. The Hartburn flagons were bulb-shaped, moulded round the lip, with spouts and double-curved handles. The Berwick paten bore the town's arms in the centre, decorated with flowing mantling.[18]

Secular pieces were well represented, from a simple tablespoon of 1728, the first year in which he made plate, to the elaborate rose-water ewer of 1754, the year of his death. A handsome article, chased with flowers and foliage in relief, it had a mask with spiral horns under the spout, a moulded band round the centre and a terminal bust of bold design on the double-curved handle. A 1732 globular tea-kettle and stand, beautifully engraved round the top with interlaced bands and shells, an ebony handle and knop, contrasted sharply with the fashion of 1751. Cookson's mid-century kettle was pear-shaped, covered with a repoussé design of flowers, leaves and strap-work. It had ornamental shields on the sides; the spout was an eagle's head, the handle formed of two mermaids and the knop a pineapple. The stand had three shell feet, acanthus leaves round the top and an overhanging perforated rim, an excellent example of ornate Georgian work, which flatly contradicted Le Blanc's assumption. Among the cups and coffee-pots, sauce-boats, salvers, tea-caddies and tankards stood, somewhat incongruously, two bleeding-bowls. Did the sight of their perforated strap-work handles, moulded edges and base soothe the apprehensive victim of an unpleasant experience?

Cookson will always be remembered for his part in the affair of the Corbridge lanx which created a great stir at the time.

In February 1735, Isabel Cutter, the local blacksmith's nine-year-old daughter, and her playmate, Hester Skipsey, a labourer's child, were gathering sticks in a close by the river. The sharp-eyed Isabel saw a whitish object half-submerged in the gravel and sand where a small stream joins the Tyne just below the bridge. She pulled out a large dish and ran home in triumph with her new toy, as she thought. Her father had other ideas. He broke off one foot and took it to Cookson, whose offer of 36s. for this piece of silver was promptly accepted. At the beginning of March, Cutter reappeared with the plate which Cookson bought for thirty guineas, although the man would not say how he had come by it. When cleaned, it proved to be a magnificently decorated lanx. The news aroused great enthusiasm among antiquarians from Pennycuik to Spalding who were not a little anxious lest it be melted down[19] or sold abroad. They were kept informed of developments by Robert Cay of Westgate-street who, on going to inspect this rare treasure, found Cookson very reticent about

The Corbridge Lanx

By courtesy of the Museum of Antiquities of the University and the Society of Antiquaries of Newcastle upon Tyne.

his plans. He seems to have suspected that the lanx was treasure trove but disclaimed any precise knowledge of its original whereabouts. He would not say from whom he had bought it but admitted that he hoped to sell it to an unspecified buyer for two hundred guineas. All Cookson was prepared to do was to allow a sketch of the plate to be made for the restricted use of the antiquarians.

The lanx was not to remain long in Cookson's possession. Edward Winshipp, agent of the Duke of Somerset on whose land it was found, soon ferreted out the truth, with the result that his Grace filed a petition in chancery for the recovery of his legal property and obtained an injunction prohibiting Cookson from selling, melting down or in any way defacing the plate. Cookson was loath to part with his purchase. However, he yielded to his friends' persuasions and handed the lanx over to the Duke, who repaid Cookson what it had cost him and added a gift of money. The Cutters were summoned to appear before a manorial jury at Corbridge. In consideration of the little girl's innocence and her father's manifest ignorance of the laws governing treasure trove, a fine of sixpence was imposed.

Through marriage with the Duke of Somerset's granddaughter and heiress the Duke of Northumberland became the owner of the lanx. It is still in the possession of the present Duke and is now on loan to the British Museum. A replica is housed in the Museum of Antiquities, Newcastle University.

This episode in no way detracted from the general esteem in which Cookson was held, as is proved by the unusually long obituaries in the *Courant* and the *Journal* (August 1754). He was, they reported:

> A Tradesman of considerable Note, and of an unblemish'd Reputation. He was a Person of strict Integrity and Honour; of a peaceable and inoffensive Temper and Conduct; of great Sobriety and Temperance; and of a benevolent, generous Disposition. As a Parent and a Master, he was affectionate, kind and indulgent . . . By his Death, his Family is depriv'd of a very agreeable Head; his Relations and

Acquaintances of a most serviceable Friend; this Place of a valuable Townsman; and Society in general of a useful Member.

The press might well have added that he trained his apprentices efficiently. Among them were Stephen Buckle and George Chalmers, John Goodrich and John Langlands, who advertised in the *Journal* (5 October 1754), that they had taken over their late master's stock-in-trade and shop where they intended to carry on the business as usual.

John Langlands, son of Reynold (Reignold) Langlands, a Newcastle tanner, was baptised at St. Andrew's Church, 27 December 1715. At the age of sixteen he was bound apprentice by indenture to Isaac Cookson for ten years and was admitted free in 1754. At the end of his apprenticeship he began to work as journeyman for Cookson who was fined by the Company for employing an unfree man. Cookson was not perturbed. He had secured an industrious worker of proven ability and integrity, who was moreover good-humoured and neighbourly. Throughout his life his fund of amusing stories made him welcome in private homes and at the annual Company dinners. These were convivial occasions. A bill survives for one such reunion, held at the 'Black Boy' in the Groat Market when Richard Swarley, a friend of Langlands, was innkeeper. The meal, with a modest tip for the waiter, cost the members 30s. each, of which most went on drinks.

By 1763 Langlands had become one of the twelve principal inhabitants of St. Nicholas' parish. It was then that he was chosen—the sole representative from the Goldsmiths' Company—to serve as one of the forty-eight commissioners for the new street-lighting. Their duties were onerous and unpaid. They had to decide on the number and type of lamps, their position and time of lighting; arrange a rota of watchmen, night constables and lamp-lighters; fix their rounds, wages and allowances. A more delicate task was that of finding assessors for the rate to be levied on property owners to finance these amenities. As prospective ratepayers had the right of final appeal to the commissioners, Langlands' affability and tact must frequently have been strained.

His son and namesake, born in 1773, was admitted free by patrimony some months after his father's death in his seventy-eighth year. Langlands senior was universally esteemed and regretted. He was, in the words of the *Courant*, 'an eminent silversmith, much respected as a tradesman, admired by his friends and deservedly beloved by his relatives.' With John Robertson as partner, his widow carried on his prosperous business[20] until 1795 when young Langlands announced in the local press that the partnership with Robertson had been dissolved by mutual consent and that he was now in sole charge of the business, wholesale and retail. Unlike his father, he had a brief working life. He died, a wealthy man, in 1804. His widow continued the business for ten years and then retired to Alnwick, near her only son who farmed at Bewick. So the firm of Langlands came to an end.

Langlands senior certainly expanded Cookson's business. Between 1778 and 1784 he assayed over 10,000 ounces per annum. In the latter year he was carrying a stock of 7,305 ounces of silverware, already hall-marked, when he suffered a severe setback. The duty on silver was increased by sixpence an ounce, on gold by eight shillings. Furthermore, an additional mark—the king's head—became obligatory. Langlands also faced growing competition from the manufacturers of Sheffield plate. Boulsover's invention, originally used in button-making, was applied by Hancock (c. 1755) to candlesticks, coffee-pots and saucepans. The goods looked like silver and were immeasurably cheaper. In the 1770s machine-made plated wares came onto the market in bulk and were so popular that local goldsmiths were forced to stock them. Langlands therefore sent Robertson on a trip to London and the provinces to buy up the stock of firms going out of business. The results of his travels appeared in a long advertisement in the *Chronicle* (10 December 1785), which listed a startling assortment of cut-price goods, gold, silver and plated. He had even bought brown-ware tea and coffee urns and a wide variety of japanned articles. All were offered at a ten-day

Tankards 1780. Langlands and Robertson
By courtesy of the Director and Curator, Laing Art Gallery, Newcastle upon Tyne

auction, probably conducted by Robertson who was an experienced auctioneer.

This must have been a sore blow to the craftsman's pride, for craftsman Langlands certainly was.

Of the many pieces of church plate which Langlands made Elsdon received one of the earliest, a 1755 paten. The 1897 exhibition at the Black Gate displayed examples of his communion cups, flagons, patens and plates, dating from 1757 to 1792, the property of various churches in widely separate parts of Durham and Northumberland. All these items showed the characteristic simplicity of eighteenth-century church furnish-

Alms Dishes 1784. Langlands and Robertson

By courtesy of the Director and Curator, Laing Art Gallery, Newcastle upon Tyne

ings, whose beauty lay in grace of outline and the discreet decoration of moulded, gadrooned or beaded edges. Sometimes the plain surface was relieved by detailed engraving of the donor's coat of arms. Engravers rarely signed their work and some of the later specimens may have been executed by Beilby and Bewick, who tells us[21] that Langlands was, after 1777, their chief customer for silver engraving and that Beilby[22] was one of the best exponents of the art in the kingdom.

The comprehensive range of Langlands' domestic silver showed his ability to cater for changing fashions and to carry out intricate designs. One example was a rose-water ewer of

George II silver salver, the work of W. Beilby and J. Busfield, 1740

By courtesy of Fietscher Fotos Ltd., 5 Charlotte Square, Newcastle 1

the 1760s. The upper part had a repoussé pattern of flowers and foliage with a mask under the spout; the lower, divided by a raised moulded band, had a design of acanthus leaves, while the short stem stood on a foot chased with sea monsters and cupids. The edge was escalloped with shell ornaments; the handle was a female figure. This ewer must have held pride of place in some local beauty's dressing-room.

One of Langlands' coffee-pots is said to have graced a bishop's palace. An elegant pot and stand (1774) were known at one time as Bishop Butler's but Joseph Butler died in 1752 and John Egerton was Bishop of Durham in 1774. In 1869 Henry Philpotts presented to the See of Durham a pot and stand which according to another tradition, had belonged to Butler. The pot engraved with a bishop's mitre, has the Newcastle hall-mark for 1747–8, the year of his translation to the See, with the maker's mark of John Langlands, who was then working for Cookson. Was this indeed Bishop Butler's property and through what adventures did it pass before it eventually returned to Auckland Castle, where it is now housed?[23]

A mystery also attaches to another Langlands' coffee-pot with a ship engraved on the side. The inscription reads: 'A gift from the owners of the *Atalanta* to Mrs. Cram, 3 April 1783.' Lloyd's Register records only one *Atalanta* of that period, trading between Greenock and Great St. Kitts and first registered A 1 at Lloyd's in March 1782. Was the coffee-pot a belated memento of the launching and who was Mrs. Cram? Perhaps she was the wife of Robert Cram the sailmaker. Almost certainly she was the only woman of her day to be presented with a piece of Newcastle silverware.

The origin of the very fine Keppel Freedom Box is fully authenticated. Langlands was approached by the Brethren of Trinity House at the beginning of March 1779. The delicate work was completed before the end of April and despatched to Keppel in recognition of his many essential services to the commerce and prosperity of the country and of his honourable acquittal from the malicious and ill-founded charges of his enemies. The box is $4\frac{1}{4}$ inches wide, oval in shape. The detachable lid is engraved with a coat of arms, the reverse with the presentation inscription, the sides with naval trophies and the interior of the base with the figure of Neptune rising from the waves to present Admiral Keppel to Britannia, who is seated on the shore offering a victor's wreath. In May 1968, the box was on display at the golden jubilee exhibition of the British Antique Dealers' Association at the Victoria and Albert Museum.

Whereas Cookson's apprentices tended to work farther

Keppel Freedom Box

By courtesy of Mr. D. S. Lavender, London

Keppel Freedom Box

By courtesy of Mr. D. S. Lavender, London

afield when they were made free, Langlands' best men set up rival businesses. He met with no serious opposition either from the loquacious Stalker, who at first traded with John Mitchison but later neglected work for more congenial pursuits, or from Robert Pinkney who went into partnership with Robert Scott, another of Langlands' protégés. They advertised themselves as makers and vendors, wholesale and retail, of every kind of plate and jewellery of the latest design, but their output remained small. At first they assayed about 1,000 ounces per annum but the 1784 tax seems to have crippled them. From that date until 1790, when they dissolved partnership, the amount assayed yearly dropped to 450 ounces.

Scott then moved to Dean Street, recently opened out by the removal of the arch of the old Low Bridge and the resurfacing of the Dean, 'a place of filth and dirt', according to Sykes. This new street was to become popular with the goldsmiths.

After the dissolution of the Langlands-Robertson partnership the latter settled at 21 Dean Street with David Darling as partner for the first year and later as a neighbouring competitor. It would seem that Robertson had been making preparations well in advance for the *Advertiser* of 20 August 1791, carried the following announcement:

> Some villains wilfully attempted to burn down the new-built, unoccupied House and Shop of Mr. John Robertson, goldsmith, situated at the Foot of the Painters-heugh in Dean Street. Forty guineas reward offered for information.

Was the blaze witnessed by a young Scot, whom Robertson had welcomed to Newcastle in 1778 and who was later to trade in Dean Street—Christian Ker Reid?

Reid, the son of an Edinburgh brewer and baillie, had a frustrating journey south. He missed the regular Monday coach and had to take a devious route via Lauder, Kelso and Whittingham, reaching Newcastle on the Thursday evening, 'very much fatigued', as he wrote to his sister May. He had no intention of starting work for another week. He needed a rest after his travels and, besides, two holy days conveniently intervened. Reid was only twenty-two and clearly looked forward to exploring Newcastle before he settled down to the serious business of earning his living.

Despite his apparently reluctant début, Reid was level-headed, painstaking and determined to succeed. He gained some months' experience with Langlands and Robertson whom he found the most affable and discreet of men. Then he branched out on his own. His first place of business was in St. Nicholas' Churchyard, near the workshop of Thomas Bewick who, over the years, provided him with his bill-heads and tradesman's cards. Whitehead's *Directory* of 1790 places him in the Groat Market and eight years later he was advertising from the head of Westgate-street.[24]

On the death of his cousin Robert Ker in 1792, he had inherited estates at Hoselaw in Roxburghshire. The inheritance involved him in a series of time-consuming and expensive lawsuits which led him in 1803 to sell the property, for, it was rumoured, £9,000. He may possibly have regretted the sale as the Lowland farms enjoyed a period of unprecedented prosperity during the protracted wars with France, but he needed working capital for his expanding business which he had meanwhile transferred to Dean Street. One Peter Paxton, a far-seeing speculator, had made a handsome profit out of the deal. He had bought the site for £360 in 1789, built the premises and sold them to Reid for £1,680.

Reid was not afraid of competition from the goldsmiths already established there—David Darling and Ann, widow of the John Robertson he so much admired. With characteristic caution he made no attempt to produce showy or extravagant wares. He confined himself to small articles and concentrated on building up a reputation for turning out first-class work and for fair dealing. One of his advertisements lists the goods on sale at 15 Dean Street: tankards, pints, tureen and punch ladles, gravy, table and dessert spoons, silver shoe and knee buckles, coffee-pots, tea-pots and stands, sugar tongs and tea spoons, hair and plain gold rings.

He was possibly the only local goldsmith to accommodate the customer with a slender purse. His easy payments plan is worth quoting.

A Book is open to receive Subscriptions, at Sixpence per Week, for Articles under the Value of Ten Shillings; One Shilling for Articles from Ten Shillings to Five Pounds; from Five Pounds and upwards, One Shilling and Sixpence per Week, for which C. K. Reid will give a Promissory Note, to deliver to the Subscriber, upon the Receipt of the last Subscription, such Article or Articles as are agreed for, and which will be charged at the very lowest Price, without any Reserve whatever being made for a Discount of Two and a Half per Cent which he will allow on the Delivery of the Goods so purchased. This, compared with any other Mode of Purchase, it is presumed, will be found a very considerable saving.

Reid did more than achieve his immediate aim, more than he can ever have foreseen, for he founded the only eighteenth-century firm to span almost two centuries. Isaac Cookson had no son to carry on his name: John Langlands' only grandson became a farmer. Reid was the first of an unbroken line of goldsmiths, the last of whom retired from the board of directors in 1967, when the firm merged with the Northern Goldsmiths Group.

Christian Ker Reid took three sons into partnership and the business steadily expanded in scope and prestige. One of his most important orders was won in the face of stiff competition in 1817—a service of silver plate, worth about £1,200, which was presented to Sir Humphry Davy by the associated coal owners of Tyne and Wear at a dinner held in the 'Queen's Head'. George Lambton, M.P., who presided, paid tribute to the services their guest had rendered to the mining industry by the invention of his safety-lamp. It had been in use for two years and not one failure had been reported. In his reply Sir Humphry alluded to the 'permanent and magnificent memorial' in which the sentiments expressed by the chairman were embodied.

Had he lived to see it, Reid would assuredly have approved the removal from Dean Street to Dobson's fine new Grey

Street, long to be considered the leading commercial thoroughfare of the town. He would have been proud of the seven of his direct descendants who, in the course of the nineteenth century, became members and wardens of the Newcastle Company of Goldsmiths, the first being one of his sons, Christian Bruce Reid, apprenticed to Andrew Morrison and admitted free in 1832.

In 1854 the London goldsmiths again pressed for the abolition of the provincial companies' rights to assay and hallmark silver. On this occasion Christian John Reid and his fellow-warden, James Wakinshaw, defended Newcastle's interests before a Committee of the House of Commons with the same success that had attended Matthew Prior a century earlier. Newcastle thereby retained its privilege for another thirty years.

As Newcastle's shopping centre moved north, Reid and Sons moved with it (1906) to Blackett Street, where the business, securely based on its founders' principles, still flourishes. During the present century the firm has supplied an imposing number of presentation pieces. The most interesting are, perhaps, the superb Berwick Mace and the statue of Major-General John Lambton. This commission involved the making of a wax model from Romney's portrait and considerable research at the Imperial War Museum before the silver statue, correct in every detail, finally emerged.

It has been said more than once that only a small number of the surviving pieces of antique plate bear provincial marks and that they are largely minor items, because—it is implied—no skilled and ambitious craftsman would be content to work elsewhere than in London. A detailed study of Newcastle goldsmiths and their output, the many and varied examples of their craft to be found in public and private collections, the frequency with which choice pieces appear in today's auction rooms, would suggest that such assumptions require some modification.

NOTES

1. Between 1951 and 1968 it increased tenfold. (*The Times Saturday Review*, 12 October 1968.)
2. Gold was first assayed in Newcastle for John Mitchison of the Side, 11 March 1785.
3. He was arraigned by Sir Hugh Palliser after the naval engagement off Ushant, 27–28 July 1778.
4. Figure by courtesy of Captain E. Cottew Brown, Secretary.
5. Figure by courtesy of Mr. J. Davidson, Secretary.
6. The last assay of silver was 22 April 1884; of gold, 2 May 1884.
7. Son of William Prior, Assay Master 1722–1759, when his son succeeded him.
8. 'Taking ye Fly Coach for London, £3. 9s. od.; personal expenses, £10. 10s. od.; additional expenses in London, £3. 3s. od.'
9. The site has now been cleared.
10. *Memoirs of Thomas Bewick:* Written by himself.
11. 'In battering gold and silver gay,
    He battered seven long years away.'

    So wrote George Pickering of his drinking companion at Mistress Elliott's alehouse, William Stalker, who earned the reputation of being the most talkative goldsmith on Tyneside.
12. A George II tapering cylindrical coffee-pot by Buckle brought £780 at Sotheby's (14 November 1968).
13. *Newcastle Chronicle*, 2 August 1777.
14. The Company rescinded this ruling nine years later.
15. Hence the expression 'To take down a peg or two.'
16. He gave his name to Mosley Street.
17. *Letters on the English and French Nations* (1747 edition).
18. Ornamental drapery or scrollwork behind and around an achievement.
19. Sir John Clerk of Pennycuik wrote to Roger Gale in London (28 March 1735): 'I'll be glad to hear from you after you have seen this fine plate; 'tis well the goldsmith did not melt it down, as some modern Goths of this trade have frequently done.'
20. Letters of administration were granted to his widow, Margaret Langlands, Richard Swarley and Thomas Maddison, who were bound in the sum of £12,000.
21. *op. cit.*
22. The son of William Beilby, originally a goldsmith, who is said to have traded at one time at Scarborough. He later went to Durham.
23. This pot was displayed at the Treasures of Durham Cathedral Exhibition held in the Hatton Gallery, Newcastle University, May 1968.
24. *Newcastle Courant*, 19 May 1798.

5
MEDICAL SERVICES

Nowadays a highly complex National Health Service ministers to the needs of the sick and injured throughout the country. In our hospitals fully qualified administrators, research workers, consultants, specialists, nurses and technicians are the cogs in this gigantic and essentially impersonal machine. It is still the general practitioner who maintains that intimate personal link between physician and patient which is a vital factor in the cure of disease. Whereas the machine works inversely, the family doctor knows that his task is first to consider the patient, then the ailment.

Despite the enormous cost of this service,[1] despite all our state-controlled hospitals and clinics, there is room for similar institutions, dependent, wholly or in part, upon public charity for their continued existence. Private firms spend millions of pounds annually on research projects,[2] appeals are frequently made through the press and over the air for donations for some specific branch of medical research. The generosity of the man in the street never fails.[3] He dips willingly into his purse while, at the same time, exercising his age-old right to grumble at all and any defects, real or imagined, in the cause he supports.

Over two hundred years ago, Dr. Parker, Rector of Elswick, in his anniversary sermon for Newcastle Infirmary, gently chided this attitude:

The Scheme of this Charity hath been ordered with such Prudence, Vigilance, Integrity and Unanimity as to obtain a general Approbation: Yet, if any person think they have just Objections either against our Design or Oeconomy: fancying perhaps that it hath not all the Perfection it might have: They should do well to consider with themselves what Human Institution can be perfectly free from faults, or seeming Faults.

The grumbling goes on but, as we shall see, the spirit of individual generosity stretches back unbroken through the centuries and nowhere more so than on Tyneside.

The Barber-Surgeons' Company of Newcastle upon Tyne was incorporated in 1442 but had no permanent headquarters until 1648, when an entry in the Common Council books records a corporation grant to the Company of a site at the Manors at an annual rental of 6s. 8d., together with the stone for a building and the provision of a medical herb garden. The stone came from a demolition scheme—the dismantling of one of the finest structures in the town, the priory of the Austin Friars. An enterprising lady, who toured England in the reign of William and Mary,[4] seems to have been more impressed by the equipment than by the building. She describes with undisguised relish the convenience of the dissecting table with the chairs for the spectators, the skeletons—'the one had had the flesh boyled off and so some of ye Ligeament remained and dryed with it, and so the parts were held together by its own muscles and sinews'—and a stuffed human skin, which she had not been averse to handling.

It was indeed about this period that the Company first approached the systematic study of anatomy to improve their medical and surgical technique. One wonders how they had managed so long without it. Skeletons could be bought, the price for a good specimen rising from £6. 6s. od. in 1711 to £10 in 1891, when a gorilla's sold for £35. There was another source available, the bodies of those unfortunates who were hanged on the Town Moor. It seems ironical that those who in life had been antisocial should, after death, serve their fellow-men.

When General Guise's Highland Regiment was quartered in the town (1752), a nineteen-year-old trooper, Ewan Macdonald, fatally stabbed a man in a drunken brawl in the Bigg market. In 1764, George Stewart, a hot-tempered pawnbroker

The Barber-Surgeons' Hall at the Manors, showing statues of Aesculapius, Hippocrates, Galen and Paracelsus

Sandgate. 'The poorest and roughest district in old Newcastle.'

in Sandgate, described by John Wesley as the poorest and roughest district in old Newcastle, shot and killed a keelman, who persisted in attempts to break into his premises. Both men, like many others down the years, were condemned to death at the Assizes, hanged in public and their bodies given to the Barber-Surgeons' Company for dissection and demonstration lectures to the apprentices by well-known surgeons such as Samuel Hallowell and Richard Lambert. A macabre story went the rounds about Ewan Macdonald. The surgeons were on the point of beginning dissection when they were called away on an urgent case. On their return the corpse was sitting up begging for mercy, but a young surgeon, loth to be disappointed of some practice, seized a wooden mallet and killed him. Report has it that retribution overtook this godless young man for, soon afterwards, he was kicked to death by his own horse. The mallet was long a showpiece at the Surgeons' Hall.

Compared with all the equipment of the modern operating theatre, the instruments then in use were crude and, in the hands of quacks and tyros, must have inflicted sheer torture on the sufferer. Yet they were employed with great skill and precision by dedicated men whose sole professional qualification was a five- to seven-years' apprenticeship to a practising surgeon,[5] at a time when antisepsis and anaesthesia were unknown, when the mortality rate through the infection of wounds was 50 per cent and major operations were largely confined to the repair of injuries and the removal of limbs and external organs. The brethren had their own instruments for minor operations, such as bleeding and lancing abscesses; the others they borrowed from the Company on payment of a deposit and a guarantee that the instruments would be returned within seven days in the condition in which they were received—a very necessary safeguard, as a certain Robert Kell seems to have pawned some for 14s. and the Senior Steward was obliged to redeem them.

The Newcastle Society of Antiquaries owns a very fine collection of eighteenth-century instruments. They include an amputation knife, a finely balanced saw, very similar to those in use today, a brace and bit, lenticular knives, triangular scraper and elevator for trepanning, one of the earliest recorded operations and thought to have been performed by primitive man. There are cauteries, a curved chisel and pincers for the amputation of fingers and toes, forceps and probes for the removal of foreign bodies, a mouth-gag and spatula. Dental surgery seems to have depended upon a double-edged pelican for the extraction of teeth and a Douglas lever and punch for the removal of roots and stumps.

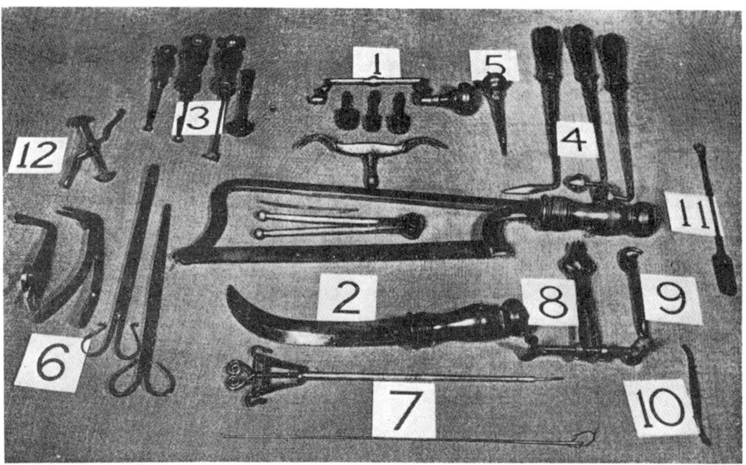

Surgical and Dental instruments of the eighteenth century, now in the Museum of the Society of Antiquaries, Newcastle

1. Trephine, brace and bits.
2. Amputation Knife and Saw.
3. Lenticular Knives, Scraper and Chisel.
4. Cauteries.
5. Punch for removal of tooth stumps.
6. Forceps.
7. Top: Instrument for removal of lead bullets.
   Below: Probe with an eye.
8. Mouth gag.
9. Douglas lever-tooth Forceps.
10. Elevator.
11. Spatula.
12. Double-ended Pelican for the extraction of teeth.

By permission of the Society of Antiquaries.

The earliest mention of a local physician is that of William de Burntof (1312), who treated the Earl of Cornwall, then in attendance upon Edward II. In the late sixteenth century, before the advent of hospitals and dispensaries, Newcastle Corporation made some provision for the care of the sick poor. In this connection the following records are of interest:

August 1592: Paide to John Colson, surgynte, for his accustomed fee for helping to cure the mamed poor folks—granted by Mr. Maior. 40s.

February 1593: Paide for the borde wages of a boy which was cutt of the stone, 4s.; paide for a strakin short (strait jacket) to him, and for sewing ytt, 16d.

October 1594: Paide to a woman sargint in parte payment 5s. for helinge 1 Anne Grensworlle of a disease, com: 2s. 10d.

Early in the seventeenth century, a town physician was appointed to the permanent corporation staff at the princely salary of £40, paid half-yearly. There were in Newcastle in the following century several graduates, chiefly of Edinburgh University, whose fame spread far beyond Tyneside. Whitehead's *Directory* (1778), was the first to publish a list of doctors. Pilgrim Street housed seven, Westgate Street three and the remaining eleven lived in the area between the Quayside and the Bigg Market. Modern general practitioners would probably consider this a reasonable number to serve a population of about 25,000. For many of them experience, based on trial and error, was their sole qualification but, judged even by present-day standards, their diagnoses were remarkably accurate.

The eighteenth-century patient suffered from much the same ailments as today's although pulmonary tuberculosis, cholera, smallpox and rabies were rife, while severe haemorrhages and lockjaw were accepted post-operative risks. The doctors, or their apprentices, made up their own infusions, tinctures and pills, relying upon a *materia medica* which varied little from that of the Middle Ages. Quinine, imported from Paris at a guinea an ounce, was just coming into use and the

Old Houses, Pilgrim Street, where Dr. John Hall was in practice

Town Moor was the convenient habitat of cardamine (presumably the large bitter-cress), extensively used in the treatment of heart diseases and for hysteria consequent upon haemorrhage.

The cure *par excellence* appears to have been blood-letting, frequently pursued with more enthusiasm than discretion. It was not unknown for a sufferer from cardiac trouble to succumb to the treatment long before his heart condition would have proved fatal. An extract from advice to apprentices runs as follows:

> if you see a patient with a hot, dry skin, bounding pulse, and a fixed pain in any part of the body, set him upright, take out your lancet and let him blood a good basinful till he grow faint; then wrap up the arm carefully and give him a pill of five grains of calomel and one grain of opium, followed by a draught of salts and senna; in a couple of hours put onto the seat of pain a dozen or two leeches and foment, or cup to eight ounces if he be strong. If no better next day, repeat the treatment, giving saline jupel every three hours.

The blue-stocking, Mrs. Elizabeth Montagu who, in 1758, was living at Carville House, Wallsend, submitted to blood-letting on the advice of the foremost physician in Newcastle, Dr. Adam Askew. While tending her mistress during a fainting-fit, her maid spilt the smelling-salts over her face. As the *eau de luce* of that day was compounded of sal ammoniac and quicklime, Mrs. Montagu was terribly burned and nearly lost her sight. A letter to her sister indicates that she passively accepted drastic cupping and was most appreciative of the care and attention she received. Dr. Askew also treated her husband's cousin for dropsy and ordered a more palatable prescription of—two bottles of hock a day.

Clad in blue coats with bright buttons, frilled shirts, thick white neckcloths, white cords and top-boots, the medical fraternity must have brought a touch of colour into the old walled town with its huddle of tumble-down houses, crowding down to the Tyne where most of the population lived. The same Mrs. Montagu complained bitterly:

> The town of Newcastle is horrible. Like the ways of thrift, it is narrow, dark and dirty. Some of the streets so steep one is forced to put a dragchain on the wheels . . . I do not know how it is that I have not yet caught a coach full of red herrings, for we scrape the city wall on which they hang with great abundance.

It was in these conditions that the doctors visited their patients. There was no hospital, no provision for people who collapsed or were injured in the street, no provision for the recurrent cases of drowning in the river.

John Pigg, Newcastle's Puritan Town Surveyor, showed his partial awareness of this problem in 1688, when he bequeathed his considerable estate in perpetuity for the relief of sickness and poverty among those who 'fear God and are of the protestant religion and have not cast themselves into poverty by their idleness nor reduced themselves to beggarye by their own riotous prodigalitie'.[6] Gradually the public conscience awakened to the need for hospital care for any sick poor and in 1735 the first provincial infirmary in England was opened in Birmingham.

Newcastle Infirmary, 1753
The foundation stone was laid on 5th September, 1751, and the completed building in use in October, 1752.

The proposal for establishing an infirmary in Newcastle is said to have originated in a social club, of which young Richard Lambert, Master of the Guild of Barber-Surgeons, was a member. He brought the suggestion to the attention of the public in a letter, written over the initials B.K.,[7] to the *Newcastle Courant* (January 1751). The immediate response was a donation from the Corporation of £100 towards the £3,697 required for the building and a site on the Forth Banks, then a four-and-a-half-acre elm-shaded recreation field with a bowling-green and terraced walks, just outside the town walls. The promoters of the scheme would not wait even for the laying of the foundation stone. They took a house in Gallowgate and opened on 23 May with seven in- and four out-patients. On that day, before a crowded congregation, which included the Mayor and Corporation, the governors and subscribers, Dr. Sharp, Archdeacon of Northumberland, preached a dedicatory sermon in St. Nicholas' Church. Taking as his theme the parable of the Good Samaritan, he delivered a competent discourse in which no one was forgotten, not even the humblest hospital servant. His listeners were reminded that everyone, whatsoever his country, creed, kindred or politics, is ones neighbour, that theoretical good-neighbourliness without practical proof is valueless, that sickness and poverty are not necessarily the consequence of sin, that it is the bounden duty of the rich and influential to help those who are not so blessed. After the service an imposing procession made its way to Gallowgate and the infirmary was officially opened. A staff of four physicians, two surgeons, a secretary, apothecary and matron, set to work under difficult conditions. The premises rapidly proved too small, so rooms were rented in near-by houses. There was no water and it had to be piped from the source supplying the Newgate Pant. Nevertheless, during the first year, 345 patients received treatment.

Meanwhile (5 September 1751), the foundation stone of the permanent building was laid by the Grand Visitor, Dr. Butler, Bishop of Durham, a generous benefactor who persuaded his life-long friend, Dr. Benson, prebendary of Durham and Bishop of Gloucester, to contribute handsomely to the funds. Sir Walter Blackett gave a donation of £1,000, from the interest on which £10 was to be the annual stipend of a hospital chaplain. Subscriptions[8] rolled in from all classes of society and, within a few months, totalled £1,200. When the poor-boxes were opened, they contained £9. 18s. 0d., and a shilling tumbled out of a scrap of paper, on which was written a ten-line poem expressing a wish since undoubtedly fulfilled:

Beneath this roof may thousands find
The greatest blessing of mankind.

Dr. Butler's sermon, preached at St. Lawrence Jewry before the Duke of Richmond, President of the London Infirmary, was later printed in Newcastle with the express purpose of encouraging further subscriptions. There were many gifts in kind, among them 47,000 bricks presented by the Bricklayers' Company, a silver chalice, flagon and Communion plate for St. Luke's Chapel and oil-paintings of the two bishops.[9]

In October 1752, the permanent building, completely equipped, was opened for the reception of patients and, with additional wards, served the town until 1906.

Dr. Butler, Lord Bishop of Durham and Grand Visitor of Newcastle Infirmary.
Painted by Taylor, a local artist

By permission of the House Governor, Royal Victoria Infirmary

It was generally agreed that this new venture was fortunate in securing the services of physicians and surgeons of some seniority and well-deserved reputation, such as Dr. Askew and Dr. Hall, Samuel Hallowell and Richard Lambert, all Tynesiders by birth or adoption. What was their contribution to the professional and social life of the century?

As doctors they shared the attributes expected of modern practitioners. They had experience which is the basis of knowledge and all the more valuable, perhaps, for being unhampered by tradition or orthodoxy; they had individuality, originality, courage, resolution. Some possessed to a marked degree those powers of leadership which reassure ones contemporaries and inspire ones pupils. They worked hard and enjoyed their leisure, rightly interpreting that term to mean indulgence in some useful pursuit for their own pleasure and satisfaction. For two of them their work and their leisure were bound up together. That is not to say that they were paragons. As private individuals they were prone to faults and foibles, sometimes dubbed typical of Northerners by critics who tend to ignore our virtues. They were self-sufficient, outspoken, never satisfied with anything but the best, cautious when confronted with new ideas, which they would not accept until they had tested them and pursued them to a logical and promising conclusion. Two were shrewd men of business but all were unstinting of their time, skill and resources in the service of friend or stranger. The old story that the question asked on Wearside: 'What are ye gannin' t' stand?' becomes, on Tyneside, 'What'll ye hev'?', neatly illustrates our inborn generosity and theirs.

Some obscurity surrounds the origins and early career of Samuel Hallowell (1709–1760), largely because of the many variants of his surname them in use—Hall*o*well, Hall*i*well, Hall*o*day, Hall*i*day. Even so, it appears a reasonable deduction that he was the son of Thomas Hallowell, apprenticed to Thomas Byerly, barber-surgeon, in whose footsteps he followed (3 June 1721). His obituary[10] states that he had a regular education and course of study and that, in his varied and extensive experience as physician and surgeon, he developed outstanding skill. There is no doubt that he was appointed senior surgeon to the new Infirmary (1751) or that he lectured to apprentices on dissections at the Barber-Surgeons' Hall. The body of Dorothy Gatonby, hanged on the Town Moor in 1754 for the murder of her illegitimate child, was allocated to him for that purpose by a vote of the Company. He was a man who dedicated his leisure to the furtherance of his professional knowledge and to the training of the younger generation. While making due allowance for the extravagant language of the notice in the *Courant*, it is clear that he devoted every care and attention to numerous pupils, many of whom were later in successful practice at the time of their teacher's death. Unhappily their names have not been recorded.

Hallowell had the engaging quality of being as ready to profit from the advice of others as he was to impart his own. He willingly adopted and carried out with success a suggestion of Richard Lambert's for suturing a vessel punctured during a phlebotomy. The accepted method of tying the artery above and below the tear resulted, in time, in its obliteration. By using Lambert's idea of a steel pin to draw the edges together with thread, a previous channel remained. When one considers that an experienced Scottish contemporary, Charles Bissett of the Military Hospital, Jamaica, published his professional findings for the benefit of his colleagues and wrote, in all seriousness:

> The fuzz-ball, I'm inclined to believe, is the most powerful styptic yet known; it hath, in many instances, within the course of my observations, restrained haemorrhages from large arteries with the aid of only a moderate compression.[11]

it is obvious that Hallowell's competence was far ahead of his times. It was a pity that the new method fell into disuse for over a century.

Either Hallowell or Lambert performed before his appreciative colleagues the first cholecystostomy at the Infirmary. In accordance with custom, the patient, relieved of a two-ounce stone, appeared before the hospital committee to tender his thanks.

Hallowell was ever ready to help in an emergency. It was October 1745. The Pretender's army was rumoured to be marching south and near panic seized Newcastle. The town gates were closed at nightfall; unauthorized people were forbidden to approach the great guns mounted on the walls; all ladders were confiscated. Many wealthy folk had fled, taking their valuables with them. A hostman,[12] William Scott, uneasy about his wife who was near her time, decided that she should be taken to her mother's home at Heworth. Without waiting for official sanction, he had her lowered over the wall in a basket and escorted across the river. A midwife safely delivered the first child,[13] but the second birth was difficult. A horseman went hot-haste to seek Dr. Askew at Whickham. Dr. Askew was spending the night in Durham. The rider galloped back to Newcastle. The gates were shut but he got a message through to Hallowell who, with a fine disregard for rules and regulations, had himself lowered over the walls, crossed the Tyne, made his way along the dark country lanes to Heworth and successfully brought into that troubled world a twin-girl, Barbara, who lived to be seventy-seven.

Such selfless concern for the sick, both in the Infirmary and in private practice, was characteristic of Hallowell, a God-fearing church-goer, who charged only moderate fees and refused to accept the voluntary offerings of his poorer patients. He won their respect and affection as he did that of his colleagues. Of his two surviving children, Jane and Samuel, the latter, at the time of his father's death, was reading for his M.D., at Edinburgh. A vacancy occurred on the Infirmary staff, which, at the urgent request of his father's friends, Richard Lambert, William Keenleyside and Henry Gibson, resident house apothecary, was kept open for the young student. He was appointed surgeon in January 1763, but died a few weeks later, just before he had completed his training.

Hallowell was equally loving and beloved in his family circle. His first wife was Mary Horsley[14] whom he married in

Town Wall. The town's defences against the Pretender's Army, 1745

1732; his second was Sarah Button, and the terms of his will prove the scrupulous fairness with which he bequeathed his property to the members of both families. The writer of the vignette in the *Courant* is careful to point out that Hallowell's moderate resources were 'the genuine and mature fruit of honest industry, not the forced produce of a rapacious appetite for gain.' Was this a barbed shaft aimed at Dr. Askew, then senior physician to the Infirmary?

A member of the Newbrough family and great-grandson of Richard Lambert, M.D., of Hexham, the fourth generation Richard early made his name as a surgeon and reached the peak of his professional reputation in the years he spent on the staff of the Infirmary (1751–1779). His skill, well-known even in London, where he had useful connections, earned for him a wide private practice, which kept him so busy that he was excused some of the duties incumbent upon him as Master of the Guild of Barber-Surgeons. He did not, however, escape the payment of a fine for unavoidable absence from a brother's funeral.

His deep interest in his work, his efforts to improve current medical services and techniques, his sympathetic attitude towards his colleagues have already been indicated by the part he played in the founding of the Infirmary and in his dealings with Hallowell. An intimate appreciation of Lambert's character[15] has been left us by a personal friend, Richard Brewster, Vicar of Stockton and a guest preacher at St. Nicholas' Church, whose sermons Lambert had evidently attended. Lambert was the forerunner of the modern general practitioner, rightly putting the sufferer's psychological reactions first and the cure of his disease second. He would spend all night at a patient's bedside to reassure him and his family. He shared their anxiety and the sound of his knock at the door was sufficient to lighten their distress. In an age when a high infant mortality rate was accepted as inevitable, Lambert showed a special affection for babies and young children, and lavished all his skill upon them. The dying and the bereaved had every cause to thank him and in the poorest homes his name became a household word.

Of the four men under discussion Richard Lambert was the most remarkable teacher. Writing in 1959, Sir Heneage Ogilvie makes this comment:[16]

> Even in teaching methods we see a tendency to pedagogy rather than apprenticeship, the only sure method by which the art of medicine can be handed on.

Lambert was well aware of this truth two hundred years ago.

As often happens, some of his pupils are remembered today when he himself is almost forgotten. On Tyneside William Ingham (1753–1817) is the best-known of Lambert's protégés. The son of a Whitby surgeon, he was apprenticed to Lambert at the age of fourteen. Ingham made great progress under the unremitting and inspired teaching of his tutor, who sent him to London to gain further experience. From that time the careers of master and pupil follow a strangely parallel course. On his return from London Lambert took Ingham into partnership in the Bigg Market. When Lambert retired from the Infirmary staff Ingham was appointed to the vacancy and rapidly became the leading Newcastle surgeon of the latter half of the century. As Lambert had been instrumental in the founding of the original Infirmary, so Ingham was the prime

William Ingham (1753–1817). Painted by Nicholson, a local artist

By permission of the House Governor, Royal Victoria Infirmary

mover in the reconstruction and extension of the hospital in 1801. Both men were noted for their wise and sympathetic handling of colleagues and patients, and Ingham[17] proved as meticulous and successful a teacher as his late master. His pupils were to be found in private practice, in the colonial service, the army and the navy.

Adam Askew (1694–1773)[18] son of a Kendal doctor and father of a registrar and fellow of the Royal College of Physicians, came to Newcastle in 1725, after graduating in medicine at St. John's College, Cambridge, and, in the course of the next fifty years, built up a highly successful practice, extending over four counties, and the reputation of being one of the foremost physicians in England.

He was appointed to the senior post at the Infirmary in 1751 and was therefore largely responsible for the establishment of good relations between the governors and house committee and the physicians and surgeons. True, there was a slight unpleasantness over the surgeons' insistence on waiving professional etiquette and themselves prescribing internal medicines for their own patients, but that little *contretemps* was settled amicably. Askew's attitude towards his juniors was not always so gracious, as we shall see. He had all the vigour and robustness of a healthy man and a certain brusqueness of manner, which he was careful to keep under control at his patients' bedside. To each sufferer he gave unfailing sympathy and care and drew upon all the resources at his command in order to alleviate their pain and effect a cure.

In private life this gentle consideration was less apparent. His lively, albeit ribald sense of humour and a ready tongue roused fierce enmity in those who were less thick-skinned. More than once in company Askew made fun of the simian nose about which Richard Dawes, Headmaster of the Royal Grammar School, was extremely sensitive. Askew went so far as to circulate among his friends a rough sketch of such a nose with the inscription: '*Non cuicunque datum est habere nasum*'. Unfortunately the document fell into Dawes' hands. He was furious and retaliated with the publication of a pamphlet, *The*

Tittle-tattle Mongers,[19] in which he castigated Dr. Askew, under the *soubriquet* of *Fungus*, for snobbery, an offensive turn of wit and abysmal ignorance of Latin. Certainly Dawes was correct in pointing out that the tag from Martial does not refer to the shape of a person's nose but to the range of his sagacity or wit. Although positively libellous in tone, the pamphlet was adjudged by a level-headed critic as imprudent but excusable in view of great provocation. There was no doubt about its effectiveness. Most of the copies were mysteriously bought up and vanished with the result that very few got into circulation. Another attack was made upon Dr. Askew in an equally outrageous document, *Will of a Certain Vicar*,[20] wherein appears the couplet:

To A—— too (by way of sport),
I give my essay upon port.

In this case, however, the doctor was in good company, for many of those mentioned in this essay, including the Corporation and Archdeacon Sharp, inherited a similar legacy. The caveat to the will comments that the general rule in Newcastle was 'the Admiration of a wealthy Fool'.

Dr. Askew was indeed wealthy. He built himself a handsome town house in Westgate Street, on the site of the White Friars' monastery, a country residence at Whickham, bought a mansion at Redheugh for his son Henry, and owned large estates in Northumberland, Durham and Westmorland. His rise to affluence was dramatic even at that time when, by lucky speculation in coal or corn, fortunes were rapidly made. He was a shrewd investor and quick to seize a passing opportunity. There is one recorded instance in which he allowed his business acumen to override professional etiquette. A country patient of means came into Newcastle to make arrangements for the sale of some property, which his attorney, also an astute business man, promptly offered to buy. While the deeds were being prepared, the patient went on to visit Dr. Askew and mentioned the transaction. Askew at once offered him £2,000 over and above the purchase price, produced pen and paper and drew up a perfectly legal deed of sale, which was signed forthwith. The attorney, not unnaturally, became abusive but the doctor remained unperturbed. 'Do you imagine,' he retorted, 'that anyone will think I have done wrong if I have cheated you, a lawyer, who have cheated all the rest of mankind?'

Dr. Askew retired in 1771 and died two years later. He had an impressive funeral with Sir Walter Blackett, Matthew Ridley and Edward Collingwood among the distinguished pall-bearers. He was buried in the family vault at St. John's Church, close to his home.

Not far away, in All Saints' churchyard at the foot of Pilgrim Street, there lies buried John Hall. In the year of the bluff, decisive Dr. Askew's retirement, Hall (1733–1793), son of a barber-surgeon and father of a future sheriff of Newcastle, was appointed physician to the Infirmary. In turn he was to become the leading doctor in the town but not before he had crossed swords with his predecessor. He was then in practice in Pilgrim Street and unconfirmed reports say that he, too, made money in commercial ventures but clearly his wealth was far inferior to Askew's. Hall appears to have been diffident in company and convinced that there was a conspiracy afoot to reduce him to a CYPHER.[21] It was a strange attitude to adopt, irreconcilable with the fact that he was first vice-president of the Newcastle Philosophical and Medical Society, president in 1787, re-elected for a further term of office, and a highly respected lecturer at the monthly meetings. Judging from his achievements, the study of medicine and the provision of amenities for his fellow-townsfolk was his life's work and recreation.

One of the questions which aroused active concern during the latter half of the eighteenth century was that of the treatment of mental disorders. In 1763 a subscription list was opened in Newcastle for the erection of a hospital for this purpose and the Corporation offered a site[22] on a ninety-nine years' lease at an annual rental of 2s. 6d. The ground, Warden's' Close, was outside the town walls between the New and West gates, with a passage-way into Gallowgate. The building,

All Saints' Church, Pilgrim Street.
Dr. John Hall was buried in the churchyard, 1793

St. Luke's House, was described as secluded, airy and healthy, with numerous conveniences for the humane treatment of the inmates. Despite the emphasis on the humanitarian aspect, there could be seen, long after the premises were converted into warehouses, the grim cells with their rings for confining violent patients. Dr. Hall was official physician to this asylum and it was not long before overcrowding necessitated some form of extension. Hall suggested adding a storey at a maximum cost of £120 to accommodate ten paying patients at £25 to £30 a year. He reckoned there would be a profit of £10 to £12 per head, which could be used for the admission of the poor. His proposal was rejected. The governors passed a resolution that only the needy be admitted and suggested that Hall should himself provide accommodation for private patients and deservedly reap the benefit of the fees.

Hall declared that, before he could make any further move, four surgeons from the Infirmary had met at Lambert's for dinner and an informal discussion on the advisability of opening a private asylum. Very belatedly they invited Hall to join them and he refused, considering his reputation would be better confirmed by his work in the municipal hospital. He then secretly bought a property, Belle Grove, on the Leazes, which he opened as a private mental home in 1766. It was to serve a radius of fifty miles and provide board, lodging and laundry on a sliding scale according to the patients' circumstances. The maximum fee was £20 per annum.

Although he later retracted his decision, Hall at first refused point-blank to allow any physician to visit his own patients. Dr. Askew was one doctor to be so rebuffed. He seems to have expressed his disapproval in no uncertain terms and Hall was moved to print a blunt comment:

> Dr. Askew's dislike to more than one of the proprietors of St. Luke's House is well known and on that account nothing civil was to be expected from him; yet in the infancy of this house, and out of respect to his age and great reputation as a physician, I would not have put a negative upon his attendance, although it would never have met with my approbation.[23]

The West Gate in 1788

Newgate. St. Luke's House stood outside the town walls between the New and West gates

Another amenity provided by Dr. Hall was the public baths outside the west wall in what we now know as Bath Lane. Neat and commodious, they were designed by Cranson, formerly an actor in the Newcastle Company of Comedians. Medicated vapour baths, 'hot, tepid or Buxton Temperature' were constructed for both sexes, together with a large, open-air swimming pool. The latter was a practical step in the right direction for there were all too many fatalities in the Tyne and discussions on methods of resuscitation, including a recommendation that some phials 'charged with the Electric Fluid' be added to the existing equipment for artificial respiration, had recently figured largely on the agenda of the Medical Society.

Then, as now, an adequate water supply for large towns was a pressing need and, in 1767, the Common Council set up a committee to consider an additional good and wholesome supply for Newcastle. By public advertisement they invited men of science, particularly analytical chemists, to look into the matter, and Hall, in collaboration with Dr. Wilson, was one of several who welcomed the challenge.

Hall, unlike some of his contemporaries, was opposed to the use of the Tyne water for domestic purposes. It was, he maintained, loaded with mud, ruined fine tea, made white meats go grey and discoloured linen. He much preferred the bubbling, delightful spring at Cock's Lodge (Coxlodge), soft water which contained alkaline salt, sea salt, a small percentage of insoluble earth and possibly, a volatile sulphur. 'We have' he said 'drunk exceedingly well-tasted tea made with it; it washes admirably, and preserves linen very well,' and he left the proprietors to cope with its rumoured disadvantage of boiling meat red. These findings, the result of six months' detailed experiments, he communicated in a lecture to the town aldermen and later published in book form (1770).

The Corporation had also taken the precaution of sending samples from various sources to Dr. Black, professor of chemistry at Edinburgh University and to Dr. Saunders, lecturer in chemistry in London. Both gentlemen supported

John Hall's views and Richard Lambert was directed to publish their report in the *Newcastle Courant* (3 November 1770).

Hallowell, Lambert, Askew, Hall and their contemporaries laboured under many and grave difficulties. Antiseptics, anaesthetics, the role of micro-organisms in the spread of infection, preventive medicine, all lay hidden in the future. There was little or no tradition to guide them in performing operations. As compensation they were secure from the dangers of stagnation. Heterodoxy had to be their watchword. For the eighteenth century they fulfilled the task commended to them by Dr. Parker when, in 1753, he preached on behalf of the Counties of Durham, Northumberland and Newcastle a sermon of thanksgiving for the success attendant upon the opening of the Infirmary. They gave freely and cheerfully of their skill to the sick, rich and poor alike; they restored the ailing to a useful life in the community; they made notable advances in the several branches of medicine; they were the founders of our local medical charities. For the benefit of future generations of doctors they recorded the results of their experience and researches, while the Philosophical and Medical Society, founded in Newcastle upon Tyne in 1786, with its lectures and discussions, helped to pave the way for the work of the British Medical Association of today.

NOTES

1. The overall running costs rose from £900,960,104 in 1961–62 to £1,490,000,000 in 1967–68. In addition, as the Secretary of State for Education and Science said in the House (2nd July 1964), total expenditure from government funds on medical research in 1963–64 (including an estimate of the support for this research by the University Grants Committee), was about £18,500,000—about 0.08 per cent of the national income for 1963. The expenditure of the Medical Research Council by grant-in-aid from the Treasury, was £7,033,000.
2. The Wellcome Foundation Ltd., and the Glaxo Laboratories each spend £1,000,000 per annum on medical research.
3. In little over a year (1963–64) the Newcastle Evening Chronicle Kidney Fund raised £31,500 by public contributions to further the work of the Urological Department of Newcastle upon Tyne General Hospital and, more recently, an anonymous donation has provided three local cancer clinics.

4. *Through England on a Side Saddle in the Time of William and Mary: being the Diary of Celia Fiennes* (London 1888).
5. Circa 1755 a certificate of attendance was issued by the Infirmary to those who had regularly been present at surgeons' practices, together with the clinical lectures therein delivered, but it was no proof of practical competence.
6. Owing to misappropriation of the funds by the trustees, Pigg's Charity did not benefit the Newcastle Infirmary until an order was made by the High Court of Chancery in 1832.
7. A ward was later named the 'B.K.'
8. Each guinea subscribed entitled the giver to recommend one in- or two out-patients.
9. The chalice, presented by Mrs. Whitfield, the flagon and plate, given by Mrs. Byne, wife of the Vicar of Ponteland, are in the possession of the Royal Victoria Infirmary. The portraits of Dr. Butler and Dr. Benson, by Taylor, and of Sir Walter Blackett, first President, by Sir Joshua Reynolds, presented in 1771, hang in the Board Room. The paintings have recently been cleaned and revarnished.
10. *Newcastle Courant* (19 January 1760).
11. *Medical Essays and Observations*, Newcastle, 1766.
12. By a statute of Henry IV (1404) hostmen were appointed by the mayor, sheriffs or bailiffs in all seaports with considerable foreign trade. The Fraternity of Free Hostmen was established by a clause in the Great Charter of Elizabeth I for the better loading and disposal of coal and stones on the Tyne.
13. Afterwards Lord Stowell, elder brother of the Earl of Eldon, Lord High Chancellor of England.
14. Daughter of the Rev. John Horsley, posthumous author of *Britannia Romana*, the first systematic study of the subject based on original research.
15. *An Elegy to the Memory of Mr. Richard Lambert.*
16. *No Miracles among Friends.*
17. The Ingham Infirmary, South Shields, was named after his youngest son, Robert Ingham, Q.C., and first M.P., for the borough.
18. He gave his name to Askew's Quay and Askew Road, Gateshead, now in process of re-development.
19. Published in Newcastle, 1747.
20. Generally thought to be the work of John Ellison, Vicar of Bedlington. Published in London, 1765.
21. The capitals are his.
22. Originally the property of the warden of Tynemouth Priory.
23. *Narrative of the Proceedings relative to the Establishment of St. Luke's House.* J. Hall, M.D., Newcastle, 1767.

6
POETS

IN 1794 Akenhead, the well-known Newcastle printer, published *A Sentimental Tour Through Newcastle*, by A Young Lady, a pseudonym which concealed the identity of Jane Harvey, the novelist. The venture was a financial success, as it was well subscribed, but the title must have sadly misled the subscribers. A *Tour* it certainly was, but almost entirely devoid of sentiment. In the short space of one week-end, the young lady, under the guidance of her genial North Country host, made an exhaustive tour of every nook and cranny in Newcastle. She was full of praise for all things Novocastrian, its hospitality, excellent fare and, surprisingly enough, its equally excellent weather. She praised its churches, hospitals and schools. 'Newcastle,' she concludes, 'is certainly in no way inferior to any provincial town in England.'

So far, so good: but one feels that the young lady devoted too much attention to bricks and mortar, to purely material matters. At one point she frankly admits this: 'The night was to me a perfect BLANK! The lives of too many of us are nothing more—but I am not writing reflections on the conduct of mankind.' Yet such reflections would have been of absorbing interest, especially if they had touched upon local celebrities. The writer comments upon the Free Grammar School and St. John's Charity School, upon St. John's churchyard, but makes only a passing reference to those who had been educated and buried there, to those who had contributed to the spiritual wealth of our town.

We find, for example, only this brief remark about one of our poets by adoption.

In this churchyard is the tomb of Mr. Cunningham, the celebrated Pastoral Poet. We paid the just tribute of a sigh to his memory.

John Cunningham, whose works ran into some sixteen editions between 1761 and 1880, is deserving of more than this laconic appreciation.

John Cunningham from a sketch by Bewick

Born in Dublin in 1729, the son of a wine-cooper and merchant, Cunningham's early ambition was to become an actor. He achieved his aim, in spite of many handicaps—an ungainly figure, an unmusical voice and a lack of the assurance necessary for such a career. He was indeed so conscious of his awkwardness that he refused to have his portrait painted, but Thomas Bewick, the local artist, was not to be gainsaid, and followed Cunningham about the town, making sketches, from which he eventually painted a likeness. Cunningham left Ireland as a strolling player to visit England, where he joined Bates' company of actors, and with them toured York, Alnwick, North Shields, Newcastle and Sunderland. An

Thomas Bewick

obituary notice, contributed by a Sunderland correspondent to the *Newcastle Chronicle* is a proof of his popularity in the district. It ends thus:

(A) passionate admiration of natural beauty, delicacy of sentiment, warmth of affection for his friends, and unaffected modesty appear through the works of this amiable poet and benevolent man, who lived greatly esteemed and died sincerely regretted by all who knew him.

His earliest work, written at the age of seventeen, was a dramatic piece, *Love in a Mist, or, The Lass of Spirit*, which ran for some nights in Dublin, and was performed once in Newcastle. Though it never appeared in London, we are told that Garrick took from it the plot of his *Lying Valet.* Garrick, according to one authority,[1] used Cunningham very ill. The latter's poems had frequently been published in the *Newcastle Chronicle* and in 1766 they were collected under the title of *Poems, Chiefly Pastoral.* Slack, whose house was always open to Cunningham, printed the collection, which the author neatly and humorously dedicated to the famous Garrick, praising his delicacy and good sense, and offering a tribute of esteem and respect. If Crawhall's account be true, then Cunningham's tribute was woefully misplaced. Cunningham is said to have walked to London to present Garrick with a copy of his work, but he met with a frigid reception from the actor, who, presenting the poet with a couple of guineas, merely remarked: 'Players, sir, as well as poets, are always poor.' In view of the fact that Garrick's name appears in the list of subscribers, this story hardly seems credible, and still less so the sequel, for Crawhall insists that this rebuff weighed so heavily upon Cunningham that he indulged too freely in Newcastle beer. *Newcastle Beer* is the title of one of the poems in the new collection. The brewers of those days evidently knew their business, for the gods forsook their nectar in its favour, Mars ordered a tun from the Sun Inn, and Apollo, tossing off a can, entertained the Muses with an extempore song. It was in fact a panacea for all ills.

You fanciful folk, for whom Physic prescribes,
Whom bolus and potion have harass'd to death,
Ye wretches, whom LAW and her ill-looking tribes,
Have hunted about 'till you're quite out of breath!
Here's shelter and ease,
No craving for fees,
No danger, no doctor, no bailiff is near!

Your spirits this raises
It cures your diseases,
There's freedom and health in our Newcastle Beer.

Critics have, on the whole, confined themselves to an appreciation of Cunningham as a pastoral poet, pointing out his fondness for lyrical descriptions of nature, his natural and simple manner, his stressing of the personal aspect, his clear, untrammelled technique, all matters of importance in considering the development of Romanticism in English poetry. There are, however, other angles from which Cunningham can be viewed, angles which appeal to local readers. Of his descriptive writing, the lines on Alnwick Castle are worth quoting in this connection.

To Alnwick's lofty seat, a sylvan scene!
To rising hills from distance doubly green,
Go—says the god of wit, my standard bear,
These are the mansions of the great and fair,
'Tis my Olympus, now, go spread my banners there.

Led by fond hope, the pointed path we trace,
And thank our patron for the flowery place;
Here—we beheld a gently waving wood!
There—we can gaze upon a wand'ring flood!
The landscape smiles! the fields gay fragrance wear!
Soft scenes are all around—refreshing air!

The *Morning Post* of October 11 1787 records the following tale.

As Mr. Cunningham, the late Pastoral Poet, was fishing on a Sunday, near Durham, the Reverend and corpulent Mr. Brown chanced to pass that way, and knowing Mr. Cunningham, austerely reproved him for breaking the Sabbath, telling him that he was doubly reprehensible, as his good sense should have taught him better. The poor poet replied: 'Reverend Sir, your external appearance says that if your dinner was at the bottom of the river, as mine is, you would angle for it—though it was a fast day, and your Saviour stood by, to rebuke you.'

The keen sense of humour here shown by Cunningham was a trait without which his life as a strolling player would have been well-nigh unbearable. Such actors often found themselves playing in barns by the light of guttering candles, with make-shift scenery and properties, and a complete lack of stage hands. It is recorded that on one occasion the leading lady was forced to announce a delay in the opening of the play as she had to take the ticket money. The audiences of those days were as critical as their modern counterparts and expressed their disapprobation with considerably less restraint. Newcastle audiences are I believe, proverbially difficult to please. Cunningham evidently appreciated this fact, for he winds up the prologue, spoken by Mr. Wallace at the opening of the New Theatre,[2] Newcastle (1748), with these words:

O that the soul of Action were but ours,
And the vast energy of vocal powers!
That we might make a grateful off'ring, fit
For those kind judges that in candour sit.
Before such judges we confess, with dread,
These new dominions we presume to tread;
Yet if you smile, we'll boldly do our best,
And have your favour to supply the rest.

What unfortunate connection, if any, Cunningham had with the legal world, I have been unable to discover, but he has more than one sly dig at the toils woven for the unwary by the law. Apart from that already noted in *Newcastle Beer*, we have the amusing fable of *The Sheep and the Bramble-Bush.*

A thick-twisted brake in the time of a storm,
  Seem'd kindly to cover a sheep:
So snug for a while he lay shelter'd and warm;
  It quietly sooth'd him asleep.
The clouds are now scatter'd, the winds are at peace,
  The sheep's to his pasture inclin'd;
But, ah! the fell thicket lays hold of his fleece,
  His coat is left forfeit behind.
My friend, who the thicket of law never try'd,
  Consider before you get in;
Tho' judgment and sentence are pass'd on your side,
  By Jove! you'll be fleec'd your skin.

This same quiet humour is revealed in Cunningham's epigraph on *Alderman W——: The History of His Life.*

That he was born, it cannot be deny'd;
He eat, drank, slept, talk'd politics, and dy'd.

Politics, too, have their place in the writings of Cunningham, who was a man of wide interests. His election ballads, contrasting the corruption of the previous century with the ideals that he sets before his contemporaries, strike a note which would not be out of place in a modern electioneering campaign.

Let the case now be alter'd, let talents be try'd;
Let national virtue alone be your guide;
Let us scorn to be biass'd by party or pelf,
And vote for our country, forgetful of self.
Let honour, let honesty, stand in our view,
To freedom be constant, to liberty true.

Though Cunningham was avowedly a party man, he does not allow party politics to obscure his vision of national patriotism. The honour and glory of England is the theme of many of his poems—*A Pastoral Hymn to Janus*, *Stanzas on the Forwardness of Spring*, *Ode Composed for the Birth-Day of the late General Lord Blakeney*, and *Stanzas on the Death of His Majesty King George II*, from which I quote the prophetic lines:

Like the fam'd Phœnix from his pyre shall spring
Successive Georges, gracious, and belov'd,
And good and glorious as the parent King.

Indeed, Cunningham goes even further and, in his *Eulogium on Masonry*, calls for the spirit which alone can give life and continuity to our twentieth century concept of a United Nations Organisation.

O! may her social rules instructive spread,
Till Truth *erect her long neglected head!*
Till, through deceitful Night, *she dart her ray,*
And beam, full glorious, in the blaze of Day!
Till man by virtuous maxims learn to move;
Till all the peopled world her laws approve,
And the whole human race be bound in brother's love.

Only once does a note of bitterness appear in Cunningham's writings and that is in his dealings with Methodism. It will be remembered that the Methodist movement became a Church in 1739, when Cunningham was a young boy, and by 1743 had shown what has been called 'the opposition of the rigidly righteous' to all forms of play-acting. On two occasions

Cunningham attacked the attitude of the Methodists towards his chosen profession. To a celebrated Methodist preacher he wrote:

Hypocrisy's son!
No more of your fun,
  A truce to fanatical raving:
Why censure the stage?
'Tis known to the age,
  That both of us thrive by—deceiving.

The attack was pressed home in a prologue spoken by Mrs. Brimyard at the opening of a little theatre at Sunderland, built on the site of a former Methodist meeting-house.

Well may the spot with meddling sprites be haunted,
Where pale Hypocrisy hath foamed and canted;
Where many a time, with insolence fanatic,
She growl'd red vengeance on the world—Dramatic;
Or, with the pencils of Deceit and Error,
For sweet Religion drew the fiend of Terror,
That with distorted looks, and rage uncivil,
Consigns her harmless neighbours to the—Devil.

Such was John Cunningham, who died in Newcastle at the age of forty-four, and was buried in St. John's Churchyard. His funeral was attended by the leading townsfolk, and his friends, the Slacks, were responsible for the erection of a tombstone, on which was inscribed:

Here lie the remains of John Cunningham. Of his excellence as a pastoral poet his works will remain a memorial for ages after this temporary tribute of esteem is in dust forgotten.

Of very different calibre was Mark Akenside, the son of a butcher, born in Newcastle in 1721 and buried in London in 1770. Akenside deeply resented both his humble birth and his lameness, which was caused, when he was seven, by a cut on his foot, made by the fall of his father's cleaver. As a youth of sixteen, he wrote a rhapsody on the miseries of a poet, born to low estate.

Poor hungry wretch!
What shall he do for life? He cannot work
With manual labour.

But 'tis in vain to rave at destiny.
Here he must rest; and brook as best he can,

To live remote from grandeur, learning, wit,
Immur'd among th'ignoble, vulgar herd
Of lowest intellect; whose stupid souls
But half inform their bodies.

Akenside was unnecessarily sensitive about his lowly birth. Had he taken the trouble to look up the family records, he would have discovered that *Akenside*, as appears from the old returns of Umfraville's land, was a tenement, or farmhold, in the west of Northumberland, from which the family took their name. For over two centuries two branches of the family were landowners and ranked as yeomen. Furthermore, he had sufficient strength of mind to carve out a career for himself and to reach that eminence of which he wrote in his poem *On the Use of Poetry*.

Yet still the self-depending soul,
Though last and least in fortune's roll,
His proper sphere commands,
And knows what nature's seal bestow'd,
And sees, before the throne of God,
The rank in which he stands.

Akenside was educated first at the Free Grammar School and then at a private academy of considerable fame, kept by William Wilson of the Close-Gate Meeting-house. At the age of eighteen Akenside went to Edinburgh to take orders as a dissenting minister. After one year's residence he changed his mind and began to study medicine. At this period he became a member of the recently formed Medical Society and distinguished himself as a debater. His ambition was apparently to enter Parliament, a career for which he began to feel much more fitted than for the profession he had chosen. Already we see signs of that mutiplicity of interests which was to characterize his whole life.

However, from Edinburgh, Akenside went to Leyden for further medical studies. There he formed a lasting friendship with Dyson, who was studying civil law and to whom Akenside was indebted for much of his subsequent ease in life. According to the *Index to English Speaking Students*, Akenside

Church of St. Mary's Hospital, part of which was converted into the Royal Grammar School

graduated at Leyden University in 1744. He published a thesis on the origin and growth of the human foetus, which attracted considerable attention, containing, as it did, new ideas upon which the medical profession was quick to act. Some say that he returned to Newcastle and set up in practice there, but they have evidently confused Mark Akenside with his elder brother Thomas, who was a Newcastle surgeon. For about eighteen months Mark Akenside practised at Nottingham, but, finding no prospects of advancement there, he returned to London, where his friend Dyson introduced him to various clubs and assemblies and allowed him £300 a year until such time as his prospects improved.

At this time Akenside was better known as a poet than as a physician. It was Dr. Johnson who remarked:

> A physician in a great city seems to be the mere plaything of fortune; his degree of reputation is, for the most part, totally casual: they that employ him, know not his excellence; they that reject him, know not his deficience. By any acute observer, who had looked on the transactions of the medical world for half a century, a very curious book might be written on the 'Fortune of Physicians'.

In Akenside's case there was also the question of divided loyalties. He was devoting an increasing proportion of his time to the writing of poetry, and his fame as a poet militated against his prestige as a doctor. Furthermore, he had an unfortunate bluntness of manner which repelled his patients. Willmott[3] says of Akenside:

> He wanted the gentleness and the patience that suffering demand: languor seldom smiled at his bidding. There happened to be at the hospital a young surgeon's dresser, to whom the poetry of Akenside was familiar, and who rejoiced in the prospect of being associated with the writer. But his hopes soon died out when he beheld the solemn and petulant Doctor in a large white wig, and wearing a long sword, preceded by a detachment of convalescents, armed with brooms to repulse any intrusive invalid, and sweep whatever dust might gather in the progress.

Nevertheless, by various stages—the award, by mandamus, of a degree at Cambridge, election to a Fellowship of the Royal Society and the Royal College of Physicians, his appointment as chief physician to St. Thomas's Hospital, as Gulstonian and Croonian Lecturer, the publication of various outstanding theses in *Medical Transactions*—Akenside eventually emerged, on the accession of George III, as Physician to the Queen.

Illustration by Birket Foster from Akenside's 'Poetical Works' (1855)

The diversity of interests apparent in Akenside's life is also clearly demonstrated in his poetry. His complete works, excluding medical writings and eighteen publications of the *Pleasures of the Imagination*, ran to twenty-two editions between 1772 and 1800. Of these the 1855 edition was charmingly illustrated by Birket Foster, himself a native of North Shields.

Of Akenside's poetical writings the *Pleasures of the Imagination* attracted much attention, and was translated twice into French, once into German, and once into Italian. He is supposed to have begun this poem at the age of seventeen while visiting his relatives at Morpeth. The work was completed in 1744 and sent to Dodsley, the well-known publisher. Akenside asked £120 for the copyright, a figure which the former thought too high. Dodsley therefore submitted the manuscript to Pope who, after perusing it, told Dodsley to make no niggardly offer as here was obviously no everyday writer. The poem duly appeared on Akenside's terms.

The *Pleasures of the Imagination* undoubtedly shows a depth of reading unusual in one so young. The author had more than a superficial knowledge of Plato and Aristotle, Longinus, Lucretius, Addison, Shaftesbury and Hutcheson. Like Cunningham's pastoral poetry, this work, with its descriptive passages, its sincere reverence, not only for God but also for nature, take its place in the history of the Romantic movement, despite adverse criticisms which began to appear after 1880.

The modern reader will find in certain passages of the *Pleasures of the Imagination* a diffuseness, a redundancy of ornament, an over-elaboration of expression which frequently lead to obscurity and to a sense of frustration. Yet it contains many passages which the twentieth century would do well to ponder. One recalls, for example, his lines on the evil effects of idleness:

Call now to mind which high capacious powers
Lie folded up in man; how far beyond
The praise of mortals, may the eternal growth
Of nature to perfection half divine
Expand the blooming soul? What pity then
Should sloth's unkindly fogs depress to earth
Her tender bosom; choke the streams of life,
And blast her spring!

With these lines contrast Akenside's belief in man's fundamental love of knowledge, and in his God-given diversity of individual talents, without which our age would never have progressed beyond the conditions of life prevailing in the eighteenth century.

For man loves knowledge, and the beams of truth
More welcome touch his understanding's eye
Than all the blandishments of sound his ear,
Than all of taste his tongue.

For since the claims
Of social life, to different labours urge
The active powers of man; with wise intent
The hand of Nature on peculiar minds
Imprints a different bias, and to each
Decrees its province in the common toil.

In spite of the fact that Akenside never lived in Newcastle after his eighteenth year, he always regarded the North Country with affection. There are several references in his early works to 'old Tyne' and to 'solitary Wansbeck's limpid stream,' while, in the year of his death, Akenside wrote:

O ye dales
Of Tyne, *and ye, most ancient woodlands! where*
Oft, as the giant flood obliquely strides,
And his banks open, and his lawns extend,
Stops short the pleased traveller to view,
Presiding o'er the scene, some rustic tow'r,
Founded by NORMAN or by SAXON hands.

In marked contrast to Cunningham, Akenside was entirely devoid of humour. It has been said of him that he had little patience for jests, and, having no wit himself, could ill brook the coarse wit of others. He appears to have shared Lord Waldegrave's opinion that a true gentleman never jests. Yet he was no mean satirist, as many of his political poems testify. In party politics Akenside, together with his friend Dyson, made an abrupt *volte-face*. Upon the accession of George III, they became as bigoted adherents of Lord Bute and the Tories as they had previously been of the opposite creed. Both thereby obtained preferment, and one wonders how Akenside reconciled his own conduct with his bitter satire on Pulteney, who sacrificed his beliefs for the empty title of Earl of Bath.

Do robes of state the guarded heart enclose
From each fair feeling human nature knows?
Can pompous titles stun the enchanted ear
To all that reason, all that sense would hear?
Else could'st thou e'er desert thy sacred post,
In such unthankful baseness to be lost?
Else could'st thou wed the emptiness of vice,
And yield thy glories at an idiot's price?

So ends Akenside's *Epistle to Curio*, which, appearing at the time of Pulteney's defection, holds a high place among English political poems, and apart from its technical excellence, expresses genuine grief at the fall of a great man and the betrayal of a great cause.

Akenside was intensely proud of England,

where freedom's equal throne
To all her valiant sons is known;
Where all are conscious of her cares,
And each the power, that rules him, shares:

O Hastings, not to all
Can ruling heaven the same endowments lend:
Yet still doth nature to her offspring call,
That to one general weal their different powers they bend,
Unenvious.

These sentiments, which are strongly reminiscent of the spirit of Cunningham's election ballads, are reiterated in Akenside's poems *On Leaving Holland*, *To the Right Reverend Benjamin Lord Bishop of Winchester*, *To the Country Gentlemen of England*. When England's honour was attacked, Akenside was the first to rush to her defence. In 1728 there appeared anonymously *A British Philippic*, which so captured public opinion that at least two folio editions followed quickly upon its publication in the *Gentleman's Magazine*. This work, whose sub-title is *Occasion'd by the Insults of the SPANIARDS, and the present Preparations for War*, was from the youthful pen of Mark Akenside. As a summons to arms this clarion call could scarcely be more stirring. In fact it created such an impression that the editors of the *Gentleman's Magazine* added this note:

. . . believing the above noble-spirited Poem will be acceptable to many not our constant readers, we have printed it in Folio, Price Six Pence. . . . And if the ingenious author will inform us how we many direct a Packet to his Hands, we will send him our acknowledgments for so great a Favour, with a Parcel of the Folio Edition.

The complete poem is too long to reproduce in its entirety, but the following extracts illustrate the patriotic ardour which inspired the whole.

Where is now
The British *spirit, generous, warm and brave,*
So frequent wont from tyranny and woe
To free the suppliant nations? Where, indeed!
If that protection, once to strangers giv'n,
Be now withheld from sons? Each nobler thought
That warm'd our sires, is lost and buried now
In luxury and av'rice. Baneful vice!
How it unmans a nation!

Come ye, great spirits, Ca'endish, Rawleigh, Blake!
And ye of later name your country's pride,
Oh! come, disperse those lazy fumes of sloth,
Teach British *hearts with* British *fires to glow!*
In wakening whispers rouze our ardent youth,
Blazon the triumphs of your better days,
Paint all the glorious scenes of rightful war,
In all its splendours; to their swelling souls
Say how ye bow'd th'insulting Spaniards' *pride,*
Say how ye thunder'd o'er their prostrate heads,
Say how ye broke their lines and fir'd their ports,
Say how not death in all its frightful shapes
Could damp your souls, or shake the great resolve
For Right and Britain.

Go, then, Britons, *forth,*
Your country's daring champions; tell your foes,
Tell them in thunders o'er their prostrate land
You were not born for slaves: Let all your deeds
Show that the sons of those immortal men,
The stars of shining story, are not slow
In virtue's path to emulate their sires,
T'assert their country's rights, avenge her sons,
And hurl the bolts of justice on her foes.

Though Akenside was a man of diverse interests, as is proved by his medical treatises, by his interesting prose work, *The*

Table of Modern Fame (1746), by the frequent classical allusions in his poems, yet we miss in his poetry the cosmopolitan outlook which characterized the writings of Cunningham. Absent, too, is any reasoned exposition of his religious beliefs. In the *Pleasures of the Imagination*, he had written, with the impetuousness of youth:

> *Others of graver mien, behold; adorn'd*
> *With holy ensigns, how sublime they move,*
> *And, bending oft their sanctimonious eyes,*
> *Take homage of the simple-minded throng,*
> *Ambassadors of heaven.*

This passage drew from Bishop Warburton the sharp rebuke that it was 'an insult on the whole body of the Christian clergy.' Akenside did not trouble to elucidate the passage but we gather from other sources that he was a deist; that he believed in a soul, but was not prepared to say whether its nature was material or immaterial; that he had, however, as he shows in his ode to the Bishop of Winchester, a profound reverence for the Christian doctrine. Sir Grey Cooper, the Newcastle-born barrister, who was Secretary to the Treasury during Lord North's administration, said that Akenside read to him a paraphrase of the *Benedicite* of his own composition, and that he was the author of one of the Christmas carols which were sung in those days about the streets of Newcastle.

Gosse once called Akenside a 'frozen Keats,' and certainly his odes never attained wide popularity. This comparative lack of success was due to a certain mental arrogance, inherent in the author, and naturally infused by him into his writings. The word portrait of Akenside, by which he lives in men's memories, is unfortunately the least flattering. It is that of the physician in *Peregrine Pickle*. Smollett, who was annoyed with Akenside for some slighting remark the latter had made about Scotland, chose the cruel revenge of inserting a satirical portrait of the doctor in his novel. As Isaac D'Israeli[4] pertinently remarks, with reference to the use of ridicule:

> When directed towards an individual, by preserving a unity of character in all its parts, it produces a fictitious personage, so

modelled on the prototype, that we know not to distinguish the true one from the false. Even with an intimate knowledge of the real object, the ambiguous image slides into our mind, for we are at least as much influenced in our opinions by our imagination as by our judgment. Hence some great characters have come down to us spotted with the taints of indelible wit.

Portrait of Akenside by Harvey

It is refreshing to notice that certain of Akenside's townsmen refused to be influenced by Smollett's embittered delineation of his character, but celebrated the centenary of the doctor's birth by assembling in the house where he was born and reciting poems specially written for the occasion. They then adjourned to the *George Tavern*, where, after dinner, a toast to 'the immortal memory of Mark Akenside, M.D.,' was proposed and drunk with enthusiasm.

Edward Chicken (1698–1746) lived and died in Newcastle, and his poetical work, of which little survives, deals exclusively with matters of interest to Novocastrians. Few details of his life have come to light. His tombstone, lying between the south wall of St. John's Church and the flagged footpath, bore the brief inscription:

> The burial place of Edward Chicken, who was twenty-five years clerk of this parish.

The records of the Incorporated Company of Weavers show that Chicken was a freeman, and that he became successively an elector, clerk, and steward of the Company. For the rest of our information we must rely upon the account of his great-niece, Miss Elizabeth Sheville, who lived in Newgate Street in 1828.

Edward Chicken had one brother and one sister. Owing to the early death of their father, who was a weaver, their widowed mother found herself in very poor circumstances, and the three children were educated at St. John's charity school, founded in 1705 by John Ord. Evidently the family had both ability and determination, for Edward became a teacher, his son went to Cambridge and was a chaplain on board the *Monmouth* when she beat the French *Foudroyant* in 1748, while his brother Robert, after taking the degree of M.A., entered the ministry. Robert Chicken never forgot the debt he owned to St. John's Charity School. In 1727 he preached a sermon on behalf of the school, in which he said:

> I myself am an instance of your readiness to promote this charitable undertaking, as I myself have felt the influence and blessed effects of your bounty. . . . It is with the utmost pleasure, and the utmost gratitude that a sense of such unmerited favours can inspire, that I now publish it to the world that the charity which we are this day met to encourage has raised me from standing in the midst of these little ones to the honour, at present, of becoming their advocate.

In spite of the fact that there were already many flourishing schools in Newcastle—St. John's, St. Andrew's and All Saints' Charity Schools, the Free (later the Royal) Grammar School, and Mr. Wilson's private academy—Edward Chicken opened another school at the White Cross in Newgate Street, where he received, as Miss Sheville says, 'the encouragement and support of many respectable families.' An excellent judge of character, and a man of infinite good humour, Edward

Chicken was frequently pressed into service by his neighbours to settle their private quarrels. His successful adjudications earned for him the well-deserved title of the Mayor of White Cross.

This shrewd sense of humour animates Chicken's best known work, *The Collier's Wedding*, originally called *A Trip to Elswick*, and variously described by local historians as 'that ludicrous and descriptive poem,' and 'one of the most interesting and descriptive local poems ever written.' Originally published about 1729, *The Collier's Wedding* went through eight editions during the next hundred years, and seven of these, all published in Newcastle, are to be found in the British Museum.

The Collier Lad and his Lass

The poem is a spirited account of the daily life and conditions of the Newcastle collier of those times. Later generations of colliers have questioned the accuracy of Chicken's tale, but there is ample evidence to corroborate his veracity.

Chicken opens with a description of the colliers' amusements, their eating, drinking and gambling, their Sunday, devoted to sleeping and gaming, but not to church-going, for they went to church only for weddings. He tells of their wives, who could drink as much as their menfolk, who left their village only for their fortnightly visit to the market on pay-day, when the colliery owners sent a waggon with them to Newcastle to bring back their purchases. Then we are introduced to the heroine, the brown-haired Jenny, on a visit to the local 'Hoppings'.

Her pliant limbs, when music play'd,
Could humour everything it said,
For when she tripped it on the plain,
To Jockey's Lost His Fellow-Swain,
Her easy steps and airy wheels
Shew'd she had music in her heels;
She danc'd so well, so very long,
She won the smock, and pleas'd the throng.

These 'Hoppings' days were usually held at Whitsuntide at some dozen places near Newcastle, and the *Local Records* for 1758 advertise the diversions to be found at Swalwell—dancing for ribbons, grinning for tobacco, women running for smocks, ass races and foot races for men.

At this point Jenny meets Tommy, a collier lad, who falls in love with her at first sight, and, after a passionate wooing at the local alehouse, is taken home by Jenny to be inspected by his prospective mother-in-law. The old woman is discovered sitting by the fire with her spinning-wheel, her petticoats turned back for fear of burning, a pot of beer within easy reach. Her greeting is scarcely encouraging.

She cry'd, 'Lass, where the de'il hae ye been?
I though thou wou'd no more be seen;
Whe's that wi' ye?—Whe should it be?'
'Sit still,' says Tom, 'it's on'y me;
I came to have a little clash.'
'Hout, lad, get hame, ye're nought but fash.'

However, when old Bessey discovers that a wedding is afoot, the atmosphere changes. Beer and tobacco circulate freely, too freely indeed, but eventually both drunk and sober go to bed.

Then comes the wedding day. The bridegroom escorted by his workmates, rides in procession along the Benwell turnpike and the air rings with the wailing of the bagpipes. The young lasses, with knots of ribbon in their hair, all bedecked with fans and fluttering favours, attend the bride.

At nine o'clock Jenny insists that they set out for church lest they be late, and the bridal procession forms up, led by two lusty collier lads. To the sound of the pipes the noisy throng reaches St. John's Church.

The gates fly open, all rush in,
The church is full with folks and din;
And all the crew, both great and small,
Behave as in a common hall.
For some, perhaps there were threescore,
Were never twice in church before;
They scamper, climb, and break the pews
To see the couple make their vows.

Then, as the couple kneel to pray, 'much unacquainted with the way,' the traditional struggle takes place for the bride's garter, which is borne in triumph round the church.

The bridegroom leading, and the bride struggling breathlessly to keep pace with him, the guests stream back to a gargantuan wedding-feast, which is causing the flustered cook considerable anxiety.

Fire, smoke and fury round her goes,
She's burnt her apron, greas'd her cloathes:
'The dinner will be spoil'd,' she cries;
'Good God! the baker's burnt the pies,
That goose will not be half enough,
The beef is old and will eat tough.
Here, lass—some flour to dredge the veal;
I wish your dinner at the de'il:
Come, take your seats and stand away,
My ladle has not room to play;
The hens and cocks are just laid down,
I never thought you'd come so soon.'

The guests are soon replete with food and beer, and the fiddlers and pipers strike up for the country dances. Even old Bessey, when she has counted the borrowed cutlery and found that none is missing, dances to the tune of *The Joyful Days Are Coming.*

At long last the festivities are over, with many of the company lamenting that the house turns round and they cannot stand. The traditional posset is drunk by bride and groom, and

Walter Blackett, from the painting by Sir Joshua Reynolds

there follows the ancient ceremony of bedding the bride.

To some the detail of the poem may seem to be grossly exaggerated, but a similar account of the marriage of William Weatherburn, pitman, of Heaton, and Elizabeth Oswald, of Gallowgate, is given in *Local Records* (1754). Furthermore, the Northumbrian poet, Thomas Whitten, has left us two poems which corroborate Chicken's account—*Johnny Breckley's*

Wedding, which took place at 'Stobby Lee,' and *The Rape of the Garter*, an account of a wedding at Hartburn Church.

Chicken's other surviving work is a political poem. The 1741 election at Newcastle was hotly contested by Walter Blackett and Matthew Ridley. A supporter of the latter wrote a virulent tract called *Is This The Truth?* in which he vilified the character of Blackett, accusing him of bribery and corruption; of failing, upon previous occasions, to promote the welfare of his constituents, and of violating his electoral promises. Chicken, who was an ardent champion of Blackett's cause, retaliated with an embittered onslaught upon Ridley—*No—This Is The Truth.*

Beginning with an attack upon Ridley's father, whom he accused of employing informers, tampering with the administration of justice, and exerting undue influence upon churches and schools—one wonders whether the author was here airing a personal grievance—Chicken reminded his readers of the old adage—like father, like son.

> *Trust not his Promises, for sure the Fruit*
> *Will be corrupted by the tainted Root.*

Then he calls upon the electors to vote for Blackett, no interloper, but a Novocastrian.

> *The great Promoter of true Liberty;*
> *The Friend and Father, Succour and Defence,*
> *Of* Nova. *Shining with sweet Excellence,*
> *Diffusing Love and Comfort where he goes;*
> *Loving to all, and loving to his Foes.*

Chicken did not have the last word in this battle of poets. Ridley's supporter launched another attack—*No—That's a Mistake*, in which he combined a slashing criticism of Chicken's poetical powers and Blackett's integrity with fulsome flattery of Matthew Ridley. This scurrilous little tract is extremely rare. As far as I have been able to discover, there are only two manuscript copies in existence, one of which can be consulted in the Newcastle upon Tyne Central Library.

To what extent Chicken's support of Blackett was effective it would be difficult to say. However, he had the satisfaction of seeing his candidate returned with 1,453 votes, while Matthew Ridley gained only 1,131. Ridley, and a fourth candidate, William Carr, petitioned against the return but failed to eject Blackett from his seat.

NOTES

1. *Old Friends with New Faces*, J. Crawhall, 1887.
2. The Turk's Head Long Room in the Bigg Market.
3. *Poetical Works of M. Akenside and J. Dyer*, R. A. Willmott, London, 1885.
4. In *Calamities and Quarrels of Authors.*

7

TWO PAINTERS

IN 1968 the population of Newcastle upon Tyne was approximately 244,880 and in the course of the year 74,627 people visited the Laing Art Gallery. These figures suggest that the modern Novocastrian's interest in painting and pictures falls short of that of his eighteenth-century forbears for whom Robert Robinson, writing on the life and times of Thomas Bewick, was full of praise.

> In the formation of that British School of Painters of which England is so justly proud, these Northern parts have borne no inconsiderable share. Though we may not have given birth to a Claude, a Berghem, or a Cuyp, or to an engraver whose work could vie with the unapproachable excellence of that of Dürer or Marc Antonio, few provincial towns in England have attained to a higher position, or rendered more important services in promoting a taste for the Fine Arts. Though much remains to be done to educate the popular mind, Newcastle has at all times, as might have been expected, attracted to herself the most promising among the youth of the neighbouring villages.

Representative of that youth were William Bell and Robert Johnson. Much of their work has survived the centuries. Some can be seen locally. Some has found its way across the Atlantic. Some is lost. Each man was entirely different in character, in his approach to art, in the development of his career, and the contacts which each made give us a broad picture of eighteenth-century life.

William Bell, born in Newcastle about 1740, was the son of a bookbinder whose accuracy and feeling for beauty were inherited by his son, later to be noted for his flowing draperies and portraits that were true likenesses. Moreover, Bell was sociable, equally at home in the society of Lord and Lady Delaval, Willie Carr, the strong man of Blyth, the Austins of theatrical fame and the members of the Royal Academy which was, in his day, a new foundation.

Bell was one of the first students to be enrolled in the Royal Academy Schools. In 1770 the Council of the Academy offered a gold medal to the student who painted the best historical picture. Bell submitted a painting but was unsuccessful. In the following year he received a gold medal from the hands of Sir Joshua Reynolds for a classical subject: *Venus Soliciting Vulcan to forge armour for her son Aeneas.* Sykes, in his *Local Records*, is rather disparaging of this success. He claims that another student painted a better picture but it was discovered that his master had touched it up, so Sir Joshua decided that it could not be considered the competitor's unaided effort and that Bell's picture, the next in merit, deserved the prize. Be that as it may, Bell certainly gained nothing but the medal for his work. Large historical pictures were too big for private purchase. Bell's was disposed of by raffle and nothing more has ever been heard of it.

Local people sat for this enormous canvas. Of these the most entertaining was the original of Vulcan, the blacksmith of the gods . . . Willie Carr, himself a blacksmith, whose harpoons were so reliable that no self-respecting whaler would sail without some. In his prime Carr was a giant of a man, 6 feet 4 inches tall, weighing 24 stones, but without an ounce of superfluous flesh. Many are the apocryphal tales that are told about him. Once he was behindhand with his famous harpoons for the *Euretta,* lying at North Shields, and the carrier left without them. Carr hoisted a hundredweight on to his back and trudged to the waiting ship. He is said to have drunk eighty-four glasses of spirit on the way and to have returned home as sober as a judge. On another occasion a customer at a public house began to make fun of Carr. Carr said nothing but quietly picked up a poker, looked at it for some time, then

William Bell

John Delaval, only son John Lord Delaval, 1756–1775. The last male heir of the Delavals

suddenly twisted it round his tormentor's neck. 'It wad hae to bide there,' he said, 'till he could behave hissel, for naebody but the man that put it there could tak it off again.'

Carr was quiet and universally respected. There was always a welcome for him at Seaton Delaval Hall, where Bell must have met him on various occasions. This was the period when Sir John (later Lord) Delaval was lavish in his hospitality and

William Bell

Susanna, daughter of Ralph Robinson of Ryton, Durham, wife of the Rt. Hon. John Lord Delaval, 1730–1783

often summoned Carr to amuse his guests, by no means all of ancient lineage, for their host was keenly interested in racing and prizefighting. When the famous pugilist, Big Ben, was there, Carr was asked to stage a fight to entertain the company. Carr agreed, came to the Hall and shook hands with his opponent, but Big Ben, watching the blood ooze from his fingers as a result of Carr's grip, declined the combat.

William Bell

The Rt. Hon. John Lord Delaval of Seaton Delaval and Ford Castle Northumberland, and Doddingham, Lincolnshire, 1728–1808

There are persistent rumours that Lord Delaval was so pleased with his protégé that he had a portrait of Carr, wearing working clothes, painted and hung in the gallery at Seaton Delaval. As Bell was at that time often at the Hall, teaching the young ladies drawing, it seems reasonable to assume that he was the artist. Tradition says that this picture was sent to Gibside. It is an established fact that there was a portrait of a

William Bell

Sophia Ann, afterwards Mrs. James,
second daughter of John, Lord Delaval

strong man in working clothes at Gibside but it was popularly supposed to be that of the local blacksmith. It was later removed to Glamis Castle and now hangs in one of the private rooms. About 2 feet 3 inches by 1 foot 6 inches, it corresponds to the description of the Delaval picture but it is unsigned. So that particular mystery remains unsolved.

Between 1770 and 1775 Bell painted full-length portraits

of Lord and Lady Delaval, of John, the last male heir, who died as a result of an accident, and of four of their six daughters, Sophia Ann, Sarah, Frances and Elizabeth. These portraits, which now hang in the Long Gallery at Seaton Delaval, are rich but subdued in colour and fully justify Bell's reputation for manipulating flowing draperies. Sophia, then eighteen, appears to be tuning a viol while the ill-fated nineteen-year-old heir has a bow and arrows and is accompanied by a little negro boy. Frances, aged twelve, and Sarah aged eight, are busily engaged in battledore and shuttlecock. Elizabeth, aged seventeen, has her harp. There they all are today, staring silently with unseeing eyes at the gallery which, in their lifetime, was full of gaiety and laughter and which looks out on to the North Front of Sir John Vanbrugh's masterpiece.

It is interesting to note that Bell, perhaps after he had put the finishing touches to the last portrait, dined with the family and the parish priest. Despite the lavish scale of hospitality at Seaton Delaval, the current housekeeper seems to have lacked originality in planning her menus. Her carefully penned records from 1772 to 1783 show that, apart from serving game in due season, she alternated between boiled rabbit and pickled salmon for dinner, no matter who the guests were. Further amusing information is to be found in the inventory of household furniture at the Hall, taken in 1801 by Robert Townson, John Raffield and Mistress Jane Sibert. Everything is listed, down to 'one duster for pictures.' The latter are all carefully counted but classified, either by the medium the artists had used or by the amount of gilt on the frames. Evidently the criterion by which the staff judged the value of the works was by size and weight. The artist was of no account. Not one artist's name is mentioned.

When in London, Bell lived either with Thickbroom, the organ-builder in the Strand, or with the Delavals at Grosvenor House. In 1775 he exhibited two pictures at the Royal Academy, a *North View* and a *South View* of Seaton Delaval Hall. Again Bell's work met with adverse comment. One critic said that the merit of these two views did not impress him sufficiently to enable him to describe them afterwards from memory. There are, at Doddington Hall in Lincolnshire, two such views, unsigned, but answering to the description of those exhibited at the Academy. Lord Delaval succeeded to Doddington Pigot on his mother's death and it is possible that these pictures are indeed Bell's work, for he certainly painted them at Grosvenor House and Lord Delaval may well have sent them to his Lincolnshire home. You can see today, in the Plan Room at Seaton Delaval, four large oil-paintings of the Hall, executed in the eighteenth century. They are unsigned and there is no evidence that they are Bell's work. They were ordered by Vanbrugh and look like an artist's conception of the architect's elevations.

The last work Bell painted in London and exhibited at the Free Society of Artists was another large historical picture, *Susannah and the Two Elders*. Bell then came back to Newcastle and Lord Delaval guaranteed him a cottage and a pension of fifty pounds a year. He opened a drawing school in Back Row and devoted his own skill for the most part to portrait painting.

Among these portraits, all extremely accurate and beautifully finished, was one of Thomas Bewick. William Bewick, of lesser fame, wrote in 1864 from his home at Haughton Hall, near Darlington:

> The portrait of Thomas Bewick that I possess was painted by Bell, in the style of Rembrandt, with the hat on, the light falling on one cheek and the side of the nose; and this, with the white neckcloth and frill, is the only light in the picture. It is artistical, but not a domestic picture by any means, and no one would like a family likeness to be so treated. But it is well painted and I am often asked if it is a Rembrandt.

It happened only too frequently to painters of this period that, if they did not sign their work, it was attributed to one or other of the well-known masters.

The whereabouts of this picture is now unknown and much of Bell's work has suffered a similar fate. Two of his portraits, *William Bell* and *Two Children with a Lamb*, eventually found their way to the Ehrich Galleries, New York City, which no longer exist. They may be in the possession of a private collector but all trace of the sale is lost. There are photographs of both pictures in the National Gallery of Art, Washington, and in London, at the Courtauld Institute of Art, who have, in addition, copies of two interesting portraits of well-known figures in eighteenth-century Newcastle, Joseph Austin and his wife.

The originals formed part of Dr. Philip Norman's collection. That of Joseph Austin is the only known portrait of the actor, who is not represented in the large collection at the Garrick Club, although he was employed at Drury Lane, not only as an actor, but as prompter and assistant stage-manager to Garrick. In Bell's painting he appears as a man about fifty years old, dressed in a red coat and a grey wig. In his right hand he holds a letter inscribed 'W. Bell pinxit, 1778.' His wife is much younger. Dark curls fall to her shoulders and she wears a quite remarkable hat, but she wears it, and her muslin fichu and flowered satin gown, with the utmost unconcern. We do not know who commissioned the portraits but the work brought Bell into a very different milieu from that to which he had been accustomed.

The Austins appeared frequently on the Newcastle stage between 1774 and 1778. Dramatic performances were, by Act of Parliament, illegal but in Newcastle, as elsewhere, managers found a way to circumvent the law. In the *Newcastle Chronicle* (2 April 1774) we read:

> At the theatre in the Bigg Market on Friday evening, being April 8, will be performed a concert of music for the benefit of Miss Pattison . . . Between the parts of the concert will be presented (gratis) a tragedy called *Hamlet, Prince of Denmark*. Hamlet . . . Mr. Austin . . .

So simple was it to evade the Act. In 1788 the new Theatre Royal was opened in Mosley Street. It was designed by David Stephenson, the architect of All Saints' Church and founder of the Literary and Philosophical Society. Joseph Austin acted on the opening night when the bill of fare included *The Way to Keep Him* and *A Peep into the Seraglio*. Two days before the

The Theatre Royal in Mosley Street. From the 'Theatric Tourist', 1804

opening the *Newcastle Chronicle* published a caustic paragraph.

The new theatre in the town will be opened on Monday evening by Messrs. Austin and Whitlock's company, which appears to have been strengthened by the addition of several new names, but we are sorry it has not been improved by the absence of several old ones.

Did Austin feel that his was one of the old names whose absence would improve the company? Was that why he retired at the end of the season and went to live near Chester? Perhaps the portraits were presented to him by well-wishers to mark his approaching retirement. Certainly the theatrical critic of the *Chronicle* would not be among the subscribers but, if Austin failed to get an honourable mention from the local press, he had the distinction of being the last survivor of the actors named in the *Rosciad*: 'Austin would always rustle in french silk.'[1]

Portrait-painting might satisfy the artist's creative urge but was not a paying proposition and Bell was forced to eke out his income by restoring pictures. He is said to have repaired very successfully the pictures in the Guildhall, which included a portrait of Charles II. They were damaged by a fire which spread, in 1791, from some warehouses at the head of the quay to the roof of the Exchange.

At this point in his career Bell faded into obscurity. We know neither when he died, nor where he was buried nor whether he left anyone to mourn his death, which occurred about 1804. If Bell's passing went unnoticed, Robert Johnson, by contrast, had friends, admirers and relatives to keep his memory green.

Johnson was born at Shotley in 1770, the only son of an aged joiner and cabinet-maker. In his youth he showed great ability at drawing and his parents moved to Gateshead where they considered he would have better opportunities of developing his art. An unnamed lady in Newcastle paid his fees for advanced drawing lessons and Thomas Bewick's mother, who knew the Johnsons, persuaded her son to take the lad as an apprentice, although he was then eighteen. The Bewick family took a great interest in the new pupil. Miss Isabella used to talk of him in the most kindly terms and tell how he would carry her in his arms when she was a child and bring offerings to their home on the Forth on a Sunday afternoon. Bewick, who was self-taught, was a good teacher. His daughter said that her father took uncommon pains with Johnson, who had refined taste, originality in his designs, the ability to portray scenes from nature and an unfailing regard for perspective. Bewick trained him in line drawing and engraving but Johnson developed, in his leisure hours, the art of water-colour painting on which his fame rests today.

So Johnson's career began when Bell's was ending. He aimed high and was not easily satisfied with his results but there is no doubt that he was one of Bewick's cleverest pupils. Among them was kind-hearted Charlton Nesbit, who was to prove a staunch friend to Johnson on more than one occasion and particularly on his death when, for the benefit of the dead man's indigent parents, he made an engraving on wood of Johnson's water-colour of Saint Nicholas' Church from the North. It was at that time one of the largest ever made, as it

St. Nicholas' Church, North View

By courtesy of the Director and Curator, Laing Art Gallery, Newcastle upon Tyne

measured 15 inches by 12 inches with the border, and was cut on twelve separate pieces of box, cramped together and mounted on an iron plate to prevent warping. Johnson's water-colour was equally outstanding, not only from the artistic point of view, but also because it was the only drawing of the North side of the church. Welford goes so far as to say that Johnson's claim to a place among men of mark rests upon this picture alone. The original is now in the Laing Art Gallery, which also has a sketch of Johnson's, a North-West view of the gateway, Bamburgh Castle, executed in 1795 and probably the last local view he painted. On the back are pasted two documents. One was written by John Fenwick to certify that it is the original and is dated 1857. The other is in the handwriting of Joseph Crawhall and states that he bought the picture at the sale of Fenwick's collection on 31 January 1867, when it was in its original gilt and black-edged frame.

The Gateway, Bamburgh Castle
By courtesy of the Director and Curator, Laing Art Gallery, Newcastle upon Tyne.

At the same sale he purchased two views of Warkworth Castle, one of Black Friars, one of Tanfield Arch and a small oval of Ovingham churchyard, all by Robert Johnson and all for the sum of £31.

Thomas Bewick and Johnson were not always on the best of terms. One cause of dissension was the authorship of some of the illustrations for Bewick's *Select Fables*, his *History of British Birds* and his *History of Quadrupeds*. It is true that Johnson had the qualities which go to the making of a good fabulist and of a good illustrator of fables. He could unite various incidents in one design, he could give those incidents a genuine basis in nature, he could delineate men and beasts, mountains, trees and rivers and he could achieve an impression of simplicity. It is, however, an indisputable fact that the *Select Fables* were published by the Newcastle bookseller, Thomas Saint, in 1784, at least four years before Johnson was apprenticed to Bewick. Thomas Wake, in his centenary appreciation of Bewick (1928) declared that the designs for the *Birds*, of which three are in the Hancock Museum, are unmistakably by Bewick. He adds that, while credit for these designs must be given to the teacher, Johnson was an exceedingly clever pupil, in many respects a better artist than the master. Bewick himself vigorously denied the claim that Johnson drew any of the illustrations for the *Quadrupeds*, affirming that the whole of those cuts were designed, drawn and engraved by himself and that he received no assistance from anyone, except that some of the trifling ornaments or tail-pieces were left to be cut by the pupils. He spoke in a friendly tone of Johnson and of himself as the victim of 'associated malice and envy.'

There is one well-authenticated occasion on which Bewick and Johnson collaborated and this was for the illustrations for Parnell's new edition of Goldsmith's poems, *The Traveller*, *The Deserted Village* and *The Hermit* (1795). Bewick drew and engraved the fine large cut of the *Sad Historian* and Johnson designed what were considered the most important and were certainly the largest, *The Hermit*, *Angel and Guide* and *The Departure*. He also drew a charming vignette which appears on the title page of the second volume of Cooke's edition of Gay's poems (1804). It illustrates the forty-fifth fable: *A rose he plucked, he gazed; admired.* The original drawing seems to have been acquired by Luke Clennell and presented by him to his father-in-law, Charles Warren, who made the engraving.

Bewick had shown his sympathetic understanding in his attitude towards the arguments over the authorship of the illustrations for his own books, arguments which were not instigated by Johnson, but he appears in a much less pleasing light in another matter in which he opposed his apprentice. In his *Memoir* Bewick talks obscurely of the envy and ingratitude of some of his pupils. Perhaps he was hinting at the incident which forced him into the Sheriff's Court in 1795. Apparently Johnson carried a portfolio of his water-colours about with him and the Earl of Bute saw them when he visited Bewick's workshop. The Earl was so much impressed by Johnson's sketches that he bought a selection for which he paid £50. Bewick and his partner, Beilby, claimed the money as having been earned by their apprentice in the course of his

Robert Johnson

The Hermit, Angel and Guide

training. Now Johnson's training did not include such instruction and he was persuaded by friends, notably Charlton Nesbit, to take his case to court. The court found for the plaintiff and Bewick and Beilby emerged the poorer by £9. 10s. 11d., the costs awarded against them.

Shortly after this dispute Johnson set up on his own as a copper-plate engraver at the head of Dean Street. Although he had been advised, for the sake of his future success, to move to London, he decided to stay in Newcastle and he appears to have done so well, despite reports to the contrary, that he was able to persuade his ailing father to retire and to support both his parents. To this period belong his drawing and copper-plate engraving of Sunderland Bridge, then in course of construction.

Robert Johnson

The Departure

Johnson although a serious young man, was not lacking in a sense of humour and he produced some caricatures which showed much of the tact and humour of Cruickshank and enjoyed considerable popularity in their day. They were the result of an encounter with Joseph Whitfield, an Irishman by birth and a prominent book-seller, whose shop was at the North end of the Tyne bridge. Whitfield used to produce an *Annual Ladies' Pocket-Book* with an engraved frontispiece. For one number Johnson did an engraving of his drawing of Saint Nicholas' Church. Then he was persuaded to do a second engraving from an architect's design for intended alterations on the North front of the Newcastle Exchange. Johnson made a careful copy of the drawing but Whitfield objected to the finished result, complaining that there was no foreground and threatening to withhold payment unless some figures were introduced. Johnson added some figures, placing conspicuously among them a likeness of his employer, easily recognizable because he had one leg shorter than the other. The infuriated Whitfield promptly refused to pay the artist one farthing but used the engraving for his publication. Johnson had his revenge. In those days party feeling ran high in Newcastle and Whitfield was ultra-Tory in his outlook, so Johnson did three political caricatures of the bookseller. The first, *A Real Friend to his Country Begs*, portrayed Whitfield, his short leg raised, brandishing a manifesto headed *An Antidote against the Black Demon of Discord*. He wore a light blue coat, striped pink and white vest, yellow breeches, white stockings, and buckled shoes. A scroll, issuing from his mouth, adjured Britons to stand forth and sacrifice a part for the whole. This highly-coloured and extremely life-like effort so incensed the hot-tempered Irishman that he took Counsel's opinion on the advisability of prosecuting the perpetrator. He was advised to laugh the matter off and Johnson escaped a second court case but Whitfield retaliated by printing a cheaper pirated copy and so underselling Johnson. In no wise daunted, Johnson produced two more spirited caricatures, *The Asses in Danger* and *The Overthrow*. When he went on his ill-fated mision to Scotland, Charlton Nesbit continued to supply the trade with copies.

In the late summer of 1796 when Johnson had been in business on his own for about six months, he was introduced to the Morisons of Perth as a likely candidate for some work to be done at Taymouth Castle, Kenmore, the seat of the Earl of Bredalbane. The first Morison was selling books at the time of the '45 rebellion. By 1794 the firm was issuing between 20,000 and 30,000 volumes a year and stood in high repute. One work in which they were then interested was Pinkerton's projected *Iconographia Scotica*. Pinkerton was a peculiar man, perpetually short of money, unreliable in business and a thorn in the flesh to all his associates. For his *Inconographia Scotica* he required copies of Jameson's portraits. Jameson, a student of

Rubens in Antwerp and a fellow-pupil of Vandyck, was later known as the Vandyck of Scotland. Many noble Scottish families owned examples of his work but the finest collection was at Taymouth for Sir Colin Campbell of Glenorchy, the ancestor of the then Earl, had been Jameson's chief patron. Indeed, Pinkerton offended the Earl of Buchan, who suggested other portraits to illustrate his book. 'I furnished about sixty drawings,' he wrote 'some of which were by my own hand, to Pinkerton for his *Iconographia Scotica*, and procured artists and correspondents for his undertaking, but he, being in no wise skilled in the fine arts, allowed the undertaking to be bungled by the employment of incorrect and inferior engravers.'

The problem of successful engraving was to disturb Johnson who accepted Morison's commission, went to Kenmore, where he lodged in an isolated cottage, and prepared to make copies of nineteen Jameson portraits. At the beginning of his stay the family were in residence and saw that he was properly cared for and did not overwork. It is evident from Johnson's letters to Pinkerton[2] that he was keenly interested in his task and anxious to produce the most suitable drawings for the purpose.

I hope the drawings I take will give satisfaction: but, as I am a little curious, I hope you will have the goodness to favour me with a few particulars concerning the nature of the publication for which they are intended, and also the style of engraving adopted for them; as it would, in a great measure, obviate some little uneasiness I have on that head, and regulate my manner of doing them in conformity with your purpose. In my opinion they should be engraved (at least some of them) as much as possible in the manner of Houbraken's heads; as that sketchy, soft, close-stroked kind of engraving is the most beautiful and suitable representative of drawings, or old, sunk-in, indeterminate pictures, which a naked harsh outline, though sought with the most difficult accuracy, can but faintly express.

The letter went on:

Mr. Morison informs me that he understands they are to be engraved by first-rate artists in London: if this is the case, I would like to take the utmost pains with them, whatever may be my reward, and would wish to know whether the name of the delineator is put to the prints; being conscious of the very minute attention I pay to the resemblance of the originals. I hazard it to your judgment in excusing such boldness; and what I means to say is, that except the engravings are done with judicious exactness for these drawings, I beg you will not put my name to them. . . . From the price I have undertaken to do these at, and the *loose open sketching* mentioned in yours, a thought struck me that a less laborious kind of drawing, with sufficient accuracy, (which I flatter myself able to do), might answer your purpose as well or, perhaps, better.

It is doubtful whether Johnson would ever have got the fee he mentions, for other artists engaged on the same work complained bitterly that they had never received their very modest reward . . . half a guinea for an outline, one guinea for a sketch in India ink, one guinea and a half for a coloured sketch. Johnson would certainly have been dissatisfied with the quality of the engraving which led one critic to comment that the portraits were so bad as to be a disgrace to the arts in England.

Johnson was never to hear this condemnation. The family had left Taymouth and Johnson, working without their kindly supervision, sat for six and seven hours at a stretch in an unheated parlour, in his anxiety to finish the work. He had done fifteen sketches when he succumbed to a fever. His landlord, confusing delirium with madness, had him bound and beaten. Fortunately, the day before he died, a Doctor M'Lagen happened to pass through Kenmore and he released Johnson from his bonds and did what little he could to relieve his suffering. Mr. Morison, distressed by this tragic death, for he had formed an affection for one whom he deemed a deserving young man of the most exemplary character, arranged for his burial and paid the expenses. Morison tells us that an unknown young man came from Newcastle to collect Johnson's belongings. Was it his friend, Charlton Nesbit? Nesbit cut a memorial in wood from one of his own designs and made a limited number of impressions. It was a scene of a country churchyard by moonlight, with a weeping woman leaning on a tombstone, and it was inscribed: 'In memory of R. Johnson,

1796.' His friends later erected a stone to his memory on the south side of Ovingham Church, not far from the memorials to the Bewicks. Sykes, in his *Local Records*, published an effusive obituary: 'By his premature death the fine arts sustained an irreparable loss, as his genius was soaring rapidly to a pitch of the highest elegance.'

The tribute paid by his parents rings true and is affecting in its simplicity. They sent his relatives and friends a memorial card which read:

Robert Johnson of Gateshead,
Painter and Engraver

Died at Kenmore, in Perthshire, 29 October 1796. The works of his Pencil speak for themselves. His other Valuable and Pleasing Qualifications can be justly appreciated only by those who knew him.

NOTES

1. By the Rev. Charles Churchill (1731–64). Written in 1761.
2. In *Literary Correspondence* (1830 edition) by J. Pinkerton.

8

NEWCASTLE LADIES

In 428 B.C. Euripides voiced his hatred of learned women, together with the pious hope that there would never be under his roof a woman knowing more than a woman ought to know. The fulfilment, or otherwise, of this heartfelt wish is shrouded in obscurity, but it is assuredly clear what his reactions would have been to the changed status of women in our day.

Their evolution has been a very slow process. Even in the eighteenth century, Cowper in his poem *Truth*, would only venture to say that learning, once the prerogative of men, was 'verging fast towards the female side.' It must be admitted that men were loth to relinquish their prerogative. One of the early numbers of the *Spectator* gives a diverting account of the chance inspection of a lady's library. So heterogeneous was the collection that the visitor invited the subscribers to the periodical to air their views upon books suitable for inclusion in such a library. From the point of view of quantity the response was most gratifying but the quality left much to be desired. Booksellers, with an eye to their own advantage and complete disregard for the general education of women, cried their own wares, and suggested Dalton's *Country Justice*, *The Compleat Jockey*, Bayle's *Dictionary* or *Mr. Mede upon the Revelations*, the latter to satisfy woman's innate curiosity and proneness to pry into secrets. Husbands, if the writers may be believed, would have had their wives read *A Dissuasive from the Playhouse*, *The Pleasures of a Country Life*, *The Government of the Tongue*, *Wingate's Arithmetic* and *The Countess of Kent's Receipts*. Their wives were, in short, to be efficient, contented, quiet chatelaines and nothing more. Men of learning neatly avoided committing themselves by ponderously stating that they must be given time to examine a multitude of books before they could make any concrete suggestions.

Indifference and opposition retarded, but did not put a stop to, the emancipation of women. The ladies of Newcastle upon Tyne, among them Mrs. Elstob, Mrs. Gomeldon and Mrs. Slack, can lay claim to their share in the feminist movement.

When Mrs. Elstob's contributions to learned literature were in preparation, England was ruled by Queen Anne. The victories of Blenheim, Ramillies and Oudenarde, the capture of Gibraltar, had added to the prestige of our armed forces. At home the Union of England and Scotland had been effected; the question of the succession became of paramount importance and the reign ended in the midst of party strife. In these events Novocastrians took their part. Vice-admiral Sir Ralph Delaval acquitted himself nobly in the naval victory off the Hague. The Corporation of Newcastle dutifully presented the Queen with an address of congratulations on the happy union of the two kingdoms, and later rejoiced in another union between England and Scotland, which brought fresh business to the town—the running of the new Edinburgh, Berwick, Newcastle, Durham and London stage-coach (1712), which performed the journey in the incredibly short space of thirteen days at a cost of £4. 10s. 0d. per passenger. Three years later, under the Earl of Derwentwater, a large following proclaimed the Pretender king, and marched on Newcastle. Their advance was checked by the prompt action of the magistrates and deputy-lieutenants who blocked the gates, arrested all suspected persons, armed the inhabitants and called out the militia. They were joined by forces under the Earl of Scarborough, then lord-lieutenant of Northumberland, so that the town was full of ardent supporters of the new King George I. Those were stirring times, but their clamour failed to disturb the studies of one of the greatest Anglo-Saxon scholars England has ever known, Elizabeth Elstob.

Mrs. (a courtesy title), Elstob had her family's genealogical tree drawn up on vellum and it is still to be seen in the Harleian Collection in the British Museum. On her mother's side she claimed descent from the old kings of Wales. Her father's family had long been established near Sedgefield, but seems to have lived in comparative obscurity until her father, Ralph Elstob, settled in Newcastle upon Tyne, being numbered among the merchant adventurers of that town and becoming sheriff in 1683, the year of his famous daughter's birth. Her brother William, ten years her senior, was a pupil of the Free Grammar School and attained celebrity in the same field as Elizabeth, that of Anglo-Saxon studies.

Elizabeth inherited her love of literature from her mother and she was unfortunate in being orphaned at the early age of eight. Her uncle and guardian, Dr. Charles Elstob, presumably a scholar as well as a divine, held the current view on the education of women and declared that one tongue was enough for any female. He flatly refused to allow his niece to study any language but her own. The child, however, had determination. Indeed, a later estimate of her character indicates that she was slow but steadily progressive, qualities which often outstrip genius itself in the field of literature. Supported by her brother, whose help she never forgot and publicly acknowledged on more than one occasion, she finally obtained her uncle's permission to learn French. She proved her skill in this language by her translation of Mademoiselle de Scudéry's *Essay on Glory*, and her preparation of a French version of Roger Ascham's letters, already published in English by William Elstob. Before she died she was mistress of nine languages, including the ancient and almost obsolete Anglo-Saxon. In addition her works bear testimony to her sound knowledge of antiquities and divinity.

Mrs. Elstob did not remain long in Newcastle. She accompanied her brother first to Oxford and then to London. At the University, where she shared her brother's studies, she won the respect and admiration of Dr. Hudson and other leading Oxonians. In London she found herself in eminent society. Mr.

Thoresby, writing to Dr. Richardson,[1] mentions a visit to London and a gathering at which he had met the Archbishop of Canterbury, several bishops and various authors, lay and clerical, among them Sir Isaac Newton, then president of the Royal Society. Writers of the fair sex were there also, and Mr. Thoresby comments upon the presence of Bishop Burnet's wife and of Mrs. Elstob, evidently considering it a triumph that the latter had consented to write something in his album. Mr. Thoresby seems to have been a forerunner of the modern autograph-hunter.

Elizabeth Elstob

In 1709 Mrs. Elstob published *An English-Saxon Homily on the Birthday of Saint Gregory*, which gave an account of the conversion of the English to Christianity. Dedicated to Queen Anne it was a beautifully produced, albeit a trifle pompous book. The engravings were by Gribelin and, peering through the initial letter 'G,' was the portrait of the authoress who, unlike Mrs. Gomeldon, made no attempt to disguise her sex. Although

Mr. Thoresby gave notice of this work by the 'justly celebrated Saxon Nymph' and Ballard acclaimed it as an excellent and learned performance, which it undoubtedly was, Mrs. Elstob was uncertain of its reception. She fully realized the opposition it might arouse in the other sex and spoke bitterly in her preface:

> I know it will be said, What has a woman to do with learning? This I have known urged by some men, with an envy unbecoming that greatness of soul, which is said to dignify their sex. For if women may be said to have souls, and that their souls are their better part, and that what is best deserves our greatest care for its improvement; furthermore, if good learning be one of the soul's greatest improvements; we must retort the question Where is the fault in women seeking after learning? Why are they not to be valued for acquiring to themselves the noblest ornament? What hurt can this be to themselves? What disadvantages to learning?

She countered the two main arguments against the further education of women—that it made them impertinent and caused them to neglect their household duties—by pointing out that such a consequence is the fault of the individual, not of learning, which teaches method, regularity and greater dexterity in all directions. Of those women, who meekly acquiesced in the existing state of affairs, Mrs. Elstob was overtly contemptuous. She berated them soundly for abandoning themselves to ignorance as if they were devoid of intelligence, and warned them that their punishment was their very ignorance, whether they were sensible of it or not. Such a diatribe was not calculated to popularize her work but, strangely enough, it was still well received, particularly in the North. The list of local subscribers, among them not a few ladies, contains forty names, including those of the Vicar of Newcastle, the Rector of Gateshead and Sedgefield, the Mayor and Recorder of Newcastle, together with various aldermen and gentlemen of the district. Even Dr. Elstob, who had deliberately put every obstacle in the way of his niece's education, unbent so far as to buy a copy of the work which brought the family name into prominence.

Six years later there appeared *The Rudiments of Grammar for the English-Saxon Tongue*. The original Saxon types, used for printing the *Homily* and a specimen grammar (1712), were lost in a serious fire which destroyed her printer's works in London. Elizabeth Elstob, being an artist as well as a scholar and undaunted by difficulties, made a fresh set of facsimiles and from them Lord Chief Justice Parker had new types cut for her grammar. This was the only occasion on which they were used, and the matrices and punches were afterwards presented to Oxford University. The idea of an Anglo-Saxon Grammar had come to her some years previously when she was visiting friends at Canterbury. There she met a young lady who, to Mrs. Elstob's considerable astonishment, expressed a wish to study that ancient tongue. She was more than a little surprised that another woman should show a predilection for the abstruse study to which her own attention had first been drawn by its similarity to the dialect of Tyneside, where her childhood days were spent. The immediate result was the publication of the specimen grammar mentioned above. In the meantime she lost touch with her pupil. History does not relate how the breach occurred, but Anglo-Saxon is a notoriously difficult language to master and probably the young aspirant was discouraged. Mrs. Elstob therefore took three more years to add the final touches to the first Anglo-Saxon grammar book ever written in English. It was dedicated to Princess, later Queen, Caroline, to whom she had the honour of being presented.

Her attitude was more strongly feminist than ever. This present, she said in her dedication, worthless as it was, was the humble tribute of a female. No one was more fitted to play the part of literary critic than a woman for, whereas our worldly goods are justly called our patrimony, being the fruits of our father's industry, the language we speak is our mother tongue. So it was a woman's duty to show the men of the times that their native language was neither as barren nor as barbarous as they, with equal ignorance and boldness, affirmed. A curious contradiction in her nature made Mrs. Elstob acknowledge punctiliously her indebtedness to Mr. Thwaites and Dr. Hickes for their help in the compilation of the book.

Dr. Hickes was apparently her maternal grandfather and himself an outstanding scholar. He encouraged Mrs. Elstob to pursue an ambitious project, the *Saxon Homilarium*, which would have been the first translation into modern English of the homilies of Ælfric, Archbishop of Canterbury. Dr. Hickes, whose relationship to the authoress may have made him somewhat biased, spoke in the most glowing terms of this undertaking. It would, he declared, be of service to the Church of England and an honour to Northern learning, our Anglo-Saxon ancestors, our country and the writer's sex. The work was begun printing in folio form at Oxford and the Lord Treasurer obtained for Mrs. Elstob the Queen's bounty to help to defray expenses. Yet the *Homilarium*, which had such a prosperous beginning, was never finished. The copies of the four or five completed homilies were bought by Mr. Prince of Oxford, and one, together with the folio manuscript, was presented to the British Museum.

Mrs. Elstob's literary career had come to an abrupt conclusion, partly owing to lack of public support for the *Homilarium*, but largely owing to the death in 1715 of her brother on whom she had been dependent for her income, and above all, for inspiration. For no apparent reason she chose to settle in Evesham, but before she left London for Worcestershire, another blow fell. All her books and manuscripts were entrusted to the care of a friend with whom she thought they would be safe. The friend, however, suddenly decided to join her daughter in the West Indies and no trace of Mrs. Elstob's possessions was ever found. At Evesham, where she opened a little day-school, she led a hard, poverty-stricken life. Her weekly income from each pupil was four pence, and even in those days four pence would not buy a great amount. In 1733 Mrs. Chapone, a friend of Mrs. Montagu and Mrs. Delaney, took pity on her straitened circumstances and raised for her an annuity of twenty guineas. This kind act came to the ears of Queen Caroline, who recalled the dedication of the *Anglo-*

Saxon Grammar, took her under her royal protection and allowed her a pension of £20 per annum. In consequence Mrs. Elstob was able to engage an assistant teacher and find leisure for her own work. Again she was doomed to disappointment. She offered a manuscript to several booksellers, who were willing to publish it, but would give nothing in return except a few copies when it was printed. Mrs. Elstob indignantly refused the terms offered but submitted no more work for publication. At this point she seems to have devoted herself to her scholars, declaring it was as great an honour to teach the poor children of Evesham as to instruct the offspring of the most illustrious monarch. Her leisure hours were now given up to those pursuits considered most suitable for women. She knitted her own stockings and wove the material for her dresses.

The Arms of William and Elizabeth Elstob.
Anglo-Saxon Scholars

Mrs. Elstob was reputed to have been the last remarkable person connected with Evesham. The connection was soon to be severed. Queen Caroline died in 1737 and with her died Mrs. Elstob's pension. For another two years the latter struggled on and then she was recommended to the Dowager Duchess of Portland, at Bulstrode, who was seeking a governess for her children. Mrs. Elstob had been well acquainted with her father, the Earl of Oxford, and she secured the post. She was treated as a privileged member of the household and, judging from her letters to Mr. Ballard at this period, she was cheerful and happy. She had, however, no opportunity of pursuing her studies. The Duchess had a large family and Mrs. Elstob's stated duties were very numerous. She was to instruct the children in the principles of religion and virtue, to teach them to speak, read and understand English well, to cultivate their minds in as far as their capacities would allow, to keep them company in the house and, when her strength and health permitted, to accompany them on their walks. Writing to one of her many correspondents in 1740, she remarked that her dear little charmers allowed her scant leisure. She was genuinely attached to her new pupils and her affection did not wane with the passing years. Her favourite was Lady Margaret Bentinck, whose death in 1746 from scarlet fever, which swept through the household, is said to have hastened her own end. Mrs. Elstob was now an ailing old lady and if Mrs. Delaney spoke truly, much inclined to exaggerate her own aches and pains and belittle those of the people around her, who, nevertheless, bore with her in a most good-natured fashion. She died in the service of the Duchess in 1756 and was buried at Saint Margaret's, Westminster.[2]

Hers was a pathetic, frustrated life. For a brief space she trod the literary stage, the toast of Oxford dons and London's men of letters. Then for forty years, adverse circumstances, entirely beyond her own control, forced her to sink into obscurity. Rowe Mores unkindly described her in her old age as 'surrounded with books and dirtiness, the usual appendages of folk of learning.' Surtees' criticism was more charitable and considerably more accurate. He saw in her, clean or dirty, a most extraordinary woman, the first and last of her sex, as far as was known, who was a Saxon scholar. Elizabeth Elstob shared the fate common to most literary people of her times, poverty and posthumous recognition.

The Newcastle of the time of Mrs. Gomeldon and Mrs. Slack was a town of few shops and fewer factories. Its inhabitants numbered only 25,000. At the Mansion House, down the Close and facing the river, such notables as Sir Walter Blackett maintained semi-royal state, and Mrs. Montagu of blue-stocking fame known to her intimates as 'Fidget' because of her extraordinary physical and mental activity, kept open house at Denton Hall. Thomas Bewick was still a schoolboy; Lord Collingwood was a midshipman on board the *Shannon* and John Scott was a pupil of Mr. Moises at the Free Grammar School. George III was king, George Grenville Prime Minister. The firebrand Wilkes was courting his eventual expulsion from the House of Commons; Dr. Johnson and Boswell had just become acquainted; Goldsmith was working on the *Vicar of Wakefield*, later to be sold for a paltry sixty guineas, and Sir Joshua Reynolds had just projected the Literary Club.

Mrs. Gomeldon, who died at an advanced aged in 1780, was a member of the Middleton family and therefore of Quaker extraction. From all accounts there was little of the demure Quakeress about Miss Middleton. She was very pretty and well aware of the fact, so much so that she had a portrait of herself engraved and copies distributed among her many acquaintances. It was no modest portrait to grace the top of the piano or the mantelshelf, but a massive affair, some 15 inches by 9, which must have caused considerable embarrassment to the recipients. Beauty fades with age, but Mrs. Gomeldon circumvented this sad state of affairs as far as possible. She carefully preserved her remarkably fine teeth as they fell out with the advancing years, had them set in rings and presented the resultant novel jewellery to her circle of friends. Unfortunately there is no record of their reactions to these gifts.

Miss Middleton was very young when she married Captain Francis Gomeldon of Sir John Bruce's regiment and a friend of Mr. George Bowes, whose only daughter, Mary Eleanor, became the wife of John Lyon, ninth earl of Strathmore. Captain Gomeldon could therefore introduce his beautiful young bride, with whom he was deeply in love, to a select circle, including Sir Thomas Clavering, Sir Walter Blackett, Sir Henry Grey, Matthew Ridley and the Montagus. Apparently that high-spirited lady found her husband and his friends too sedate for she very soon left him and, as he pursued her from place to place, she donned men's clothes and went to France. There, still in male attire, she caused consternation in a convent and almost persuaded a nun to run away with her. The nun remained in seclusion but sundry relics belonging to the convent found their way back to England with Mrs. Gomeldon and were proudly displayed by her in later life. She did not return to Newcastle until after the death of her husband at the Bowes' country seat, Gibside, in 1751. Even then her love of adventure was in no wise diminished. Only ten years or so before she herself died, she fell in love with the name of James Cook and wished to accompany him on his first voyage round the world. Cook, it will be remembered, was the son of an agricultural labourer, who had migrated from his native Northumberland to Yorkshire. According to the old chroniclers, the lack of feminine society aboard ship was responsible for the eulogies uttered by Captain Cook and his fellow-explorers on the amenities of the countryside and the charms of the native women of Otoheite, which they reached in April 1769. The adventurous Mrs. Gomeldon would no doubt have enjoyed the voyage on the *Endeavour*. Special catering arrangements were made to provide fresh food and fruit juice in order to prevent an outbreak of scurvy, and the official observers to the expedition, Mr. Green, chief astronomer, Mr. (later Sir Joseph) Banks and Dr. Solander, naturalists, were cultured and intellectual men. For Mrs. Gomeldon, despite her pardonable vanity and high spirits, was an intelligent, educated woman with varied interests. She was a student of natural history and philosophy, acquainted with French, Spanish and Italian, versed in the Classics and well-read in English literature. She had always been interested in books and preferred to read them in their original tongue. Her father's views on the learning of foreign languages were diametrically opposed to those of Mrs. Elstob's uncle and guardian. His severity soon made his daughter understand more than one for she was, as she puts it, 'whipped into scholarship.'

Her philosophy of life has come down to us in a small work, *The Medley*, which she published in 1768 for the benefit of the Lying-in Hospital, the forerunner of the Princess Mary

Maternity Hospital, which had been opened in Rosemary Lane some eight years previously. The hospital did excellent work among poor, married women, but was entirely dependent upon voluntary efforts for its upkeep. The annual subscriptions for the first year amounted to eighty-seven guineas and the donations, including contributions to the charity-box, which stood in the entrance hall, bearing the inscription 'Because there was no room for her in the Inn,' totalled sixty-nine guineas. The sale of *The Medley* raised a very welcome £53, 10s. 7d. for the funds. There were nearly five hundred subscribers from every walk in life and from every part of Northumberland and Wearside. Some copies found their way to such distant places as Edinburgh, London, Gloucestershire, Bristol and Devonshire. The spirit of true Christian charity, which inspired Mrs. Gomeldon to write her book, evidently flourished in the England of 1768.

Lady Bradshaigh, who was corresponding about this time with Samuel Richardson, the novelist, was well aware that a reading female was something of a phenomenon and was much disturbed by the fear that her neighbours would learn that she was exchanging letters with a novelist. Much greater trepidation moved the majority of the female writers of the time, who dreaded to be looked down on as 'an owl among the birds' and to lose more credit among the many than they could gain with the few. Mrs. Gomeldon, authoress, bowed to convention and once again disguised her sex, but she could not forbear from caustic comments at the expense of the sex she had temporarily adopted. The commonplace duties of daughter, sister, wife and mother, she wrote, no longer contented the ladies, whose horizon was daily widening. It was therefore an additional spur to write for the gentlemen to render them fit to be their companions. Yet she seemed to think the gentlemen had a long way to go before they could attain that eminence.

I shall studiously endeavour to promote the easy Conveyance of my Ideas with fine Paper, handsome Type, large Letter, large Margin, and Ribbands to mark, proper Spaces at Top and Bottom, short

Paragraphs, and shall put as little into the Paper as I possibly can: in short, no Care shall be omitted to please the Polite.

Although she championed the cause of women, Mrs. Gomeldon was not blind to their defects. For the domineering, masculine type she had no use. The aim of her fictional character, Lady Magnesia, was to shine by perfections peculiar to men, rather than by the graces of her own sex. The earl, her husband, would, on the contrary, have made a very notable woman. He had a busy spirit, apt to interest itself particularly in domestic matters. Whether they were his own or his neighbours' was of little concern to him, provided that he had a finger in the pie. Marriage, Mrs. Gomeldon admitted, was the only career open to women in which they could direct the wills and fortunes of the other sex, but circumspection was essential in wielding such influence.

I allow the Ladies, if married, to wear the Breeches, but must beg a Petticoat be worn over them.

Mrs. Gomeldon was much exercised by a state of affairs which seems to exist at the present time, the loss of the art of conversation, and she bitterly regretted that there was no institution in being which would teach that desirable accomplishment. She therefore advised society to have recourse to Homer's maxim. Seek knowledge, which is not only the nursing mother of wisdom but of eloquence too, for wisdom and eloquence are two essentials for success in life. She warned her readers, however, that eloquence must not be confused with oratory, for the use of oratory is to inflame men's minds and the use of friendly conversation is to recreate them.

From comments upon home life and society circles Mrs. Gomeldon turned her attention to a sphere from which women were completely barred, that of politics. Her estimate of party government was brief and to the point. 'Violence is the very soul of politics.' An unfortunate condition, she thought, but one that was unavoidable, in view of the fact that the government of the day was a composition of democracy, aristocracy and monarchy. That mixture must necessarily lead every man to differ in opinion, as his political bias inclined him to one or other of those forms. On the practical side, Mrs. Gomeldon had an ingenious idea for the payment of the National Debt, which no Chancellor of the Exchequer has ever proposed, even if he has pondered it in secret.

Men value themselves upon superior Refinement: much benefit must accrue from this to a polite Nation. One Advantage in particular occurs: suppose a Tax levied upon every Man, in Proportion to his Genius, he himself giving in the Rate, and the Money raised, appropriated for the Payment of the National Debt, I doubt not but this might procure a considerable Sum, and which would also be chearfully paid.

Even more novel than the method suggested for raising tax is the conception of the cheerful taxpayer.

Many of the aphorisms taken at random from *The Medley* are not only of nation-wide but of world-wide application. They would be well worth appending to a monthly calendar, somewhat after the following fashion.

JANUARY.—'Money rules the world . . . Genius ought to.'

FEBRUARY.—'Hospitality, and the Custom of practising it would improve Society in some Respects now.'

MARCH.—'Facts are the proper basis to build Opinions upon.'

APRIL.—'The Study of Calculation tends to make rich; the Study of Books has no such Tendency.'

MAY.—'The most valuable Thing in Life, and in Science, is certainly Happiness.'

JUNE.—'There is an Elegance in Generosity. It gives with Chearfulness, and induces you to receive without feeling the Obligation.'

JULY.—'Without Action, the human Mind stagnates; without Variety, too, it grows dull.'

AUGUST.—'When the Heart is touched, we then see clearly.'

SEPTEMBER.—'The World is for the Winner; Get into Vogue, and you will push or be pushed.'

OCTOBER.—'Joke no more, for Fear of its being taken in Earnest.'

NOVEMBER.—'Prudence is a dull Sort of Quality, tho' it is of much Use to Men upon some Occasions.'

DECEMBER.—'When an old Man gets into a Vein of talking of past

Times; or when a Man retired from the World does so, there is no End to his Talking.'

Mrs. Elstob was the aloof scholar and Mrs. Gomeldon the gay society woman. Mrs. Slack, the last of the trio, successfully combined the duties of helpmate, mother and writer. Both Mrs. Slack and her equally well-known husband were Cumbrians by birth. Mrs. Slack, born in 1719, was the daughter of Henry Fisher, yeoman, of Oldscale in the parish of Lorton. Mr. Slack first came into prominence as manager for Isaac Thompson, publisher and part owner of the *Newcastle Journal* . . . the namesake but no relation of the present newspaper. In 1751 Thomas Slack married Anne Fisher at Longbenton and found in his wife an admirable supporter, shrewd and active in prospering their respective ventures. She was probably instrumental in urging her husband to establish his own paper. A difference of opinion arose between Thomas Slack and his employer in 1762. It had two immediate results. Their correspondence in the local news-sheets proved that both opponents had a very pretty command of invective. What was of lasting importance was the establishment of the *Newcastle Chronicle*, the first number of which appeared on 24 March 1764. Whereas Thompson's *Journal* went out of circulation in 1788, Slack's *Chronicle* remained in his family, under the control of his son-in-law and his descendants, for eighty-six years. It was later developed by Joseph Cowen, whose interests passed to Sir Arthur Munro Sutherland. The first number was printed in Union Street, on the site of the old Town Hall. After various migrations to Grey Street, Saint Nicholas' Buildings and Westgate Road, it is today printed and published within a stone's throw of its original office of issue.

The year before this journalistic venture began, the Slacks opened a shop, known as the *Printing Press*, at the Head of Middle Street, opposite the High Bridge. Its primary object was the sale of books but customers could also purchase perspective views, mezzotint prints, coloured or plain, and tickets and shares and chances of tickets in the current lottery. One wonders how Mr. Slack reconciled the gambler's method of making money with the financial advice which he gave in his *British Negotiator* and *Banker's Guide*. It was even possible to buy spectacles at Slack's emporium, doubtless to counteract the effects of eyestrain caused by the small type so often favoured by contemporary printers, including the Slacks themselves.

Mrs. Slack

The printing of books formed a large part of their flourishing business. The Slacks contributed handsomely to the eight hundred books printed in Newcastle upon Tyne in the course of the eighteenth century. They served private buyers and the circulating libraries, which began to spring up in the town in the 1780's. The Slacks had an excellent instrument for advertising their publications in the *Newcastle Chronicle*, of which they took full advantage. In his editorial to the first number Thomas Slack wrote as follows:

In this paper will be exhibited news, foreign and domestic, the prices of grain, stocks, et cetera, and to render it a magazine of entertainment as well as a paper of intelligence, there will frequently be inserted characters of, and extracts from, new books, with other select and original literary articles in prose and verse.

One of the local contributors of these 'original literary articles' was the poet, John Cunningham, friend and protégé of the Slacks, who stayed at their house and frequented the *Printing Press*. The latter was not merely a shop but, in addition, a literary club, where the writers, actors, artists and politicians of the district gathered together to debate current questions in a friendly atmosphere, created by the public spirit and generosity of the proprietors. They were themselves makers as well as printers and sellers of books. Mr. Slack was interested in finance, his wife in the education of the young, both privately and in schools.

It was said of her text-books that they would remain lasting monuments to her memory but the modern child would look askance at her educational methods. The trend of twentieth-century education is towards freedom from restraint, self-expression, learning the play-way. Text-books must be well-printed in clear type, attractively set out and the reading matter divided into easy sections by means of copious illustrations. Mrs. Slack did not believe in pandering to the young. With one exception, a spelling-book called the *New English Tutor*, her books were produced in close, small print, further complicated by a profusion of emphatic block capitals and italics. Moreover, the style of presentation was invariably the same. All information was conveyed in the then popular form of questions and answers, which the pupil, willy-nilly, had to sit down and learn by heart. The illustrations in the spelling-book were not calculated to arouse great enthusiasm in the young scholar's breast, being curious cuts, representing such vices as children are most addicted to and such virtues as should first be inculcated. However, Mrs. Slack declared that she had found these methods most effective from personal experience. As she was the mother of nine daughters, eight of whom survived infancy, she probably knew what she was talking about.

One of her most popular works was her *Practical New Grammar*, of which the twenty-eighth edition appeared seventeen years after the author's death, in 1795, to give the lie to a recently published piracy. In contrast to Mrs. Elstob, Mrs. Slack firmly quashed the theory that, without learning Latin or other foreign languages, it was impossible to gain a thorough knowledge of English. She stoutly averred that anyone of average ability could well be taught to write English, independently of the understanding of any other tongue, and as properly and correctly as if for the press.

Heart of Middle Street, Newcastle in 1797. Site of Slack's Printing Press

Exactly what she inferred by the last phrase is open to conjecture. Apart from the regrettable solecism, 'What do you learn grammar for?' in one of the opening questions, the student is taken adequately and relentlessly through a précis of English syntax and punctuation. The examples to be worked by the learner are, with few exceptions, highly moral in tone and most depressing material for an immature mind, which is exhorted to remember that this instant is ours, the next is in the womb of futurity and we know not what it may bring forth. An exercise in punctuation advises the student that good books are a guide to youth and an entertainment for the adult; they cheer our loneliness and keep us from being a burden to ourselves. When we are weary of the living, we may repair to the dead, who have no peevishness, pride or ulterior motive in their conversation. Talking of conversation, Mrs. Slack adds her quota to Mrs. Gomeldon's suggestions, and her remarks remain as true today as when they were first made.

> Consider your capacity, and keep within the bounds of what you know. Never talk of things you are ignorant of, unless it be for information.

There is only one glimmer of humour in the whole imposing array of examples and that is the story of a certain bishop of Escello who ordered a Latin inscription to be carved over his gate. Instead of producing, 'May this gate stand open, to no man be it shut if he be honest,' the stone-mason misplaced the comma, inserting it after 'man'. The result was a vacant bishopric.

Having mastered English grammar the pupil was ready for *The Pleasing Instructor* (1756). Mrs. Slack was not so forthright a feminist as Mrs. Elstob and Mrs. Gomeldon. Possibly the fact that she had eight daughters on her hands modified her views. She hastened to state that she would never recommend reading at the expense of sewing but that there were some governesses qualified to give instruction in both and so provide agreeable variety in the lives of young ladies. *The Pleasing Instructor* consists of three hundred and thirty pages of very small print and the reading matter, on such improving topics as the practice of virtue, cheerfulness, pride, truth and sincerity, is culled from standard periodicals like the *Guardian*, the *Spectator* and *Rambler*, or the works of Pope, Swift and Gray. An excerpt from her reprint of an essay on idleness, taken from the *Spectator*, might well be pondered by some people today, who are continually advocating extended leisure time.

If I had less leisure, I should have more; for I should then find my time distinguished into portions, some for business, and others for the indulging of pleasures.

The Young Scholar's Delight was ambitious in its scope. It contained dialogues on behaviour, on the duties and foibles of youth, on the Scriptures and the principles of Christianity, a compendium of geography and astronomy, an explanation of various arts and sciences, together with suitable prayers and devotions. The first two dialogues set out to show how a little boy could make everybody love him and how he could grow wiser than the rest of his play-fellows. He was never to be peevish, out of humour, or ill-mannered, never to look silly or shamefaced. He was always to be cheerful, ready to speak when spoken to and willing to share his possessions with his playmates. Then he was to be wise. 'Wisdom,' said Mrs. Slack, 'is to do everything that is right and to know everything that is worthy of being known.' One feels that any child who fulfilled her conditions would inevitably become a paragon or a prig.

The entire system of physical and human geography was disposed of in ninety pages. The section undertook a complete tour of the globe, including such remote regions as the Megalhanic Lands of South America, the Maldives and the Molukkos. For each country Mrs. Slack provided the latitude and longitude, frontiers, physical features, climate and vegetation. Unless a town happened to be situated on a frontier, it went unrecorded, so that the student was left with a picture of a world entirely devoid of capital cities. Nevertheless, in the author's opinion, the information given was sufficient for schoolboys to remember and to make them tolerably good geographers when they came to maturity.

Mrs. Slack's educational works fall far short of present-day standards, but they filled a long-felt want in her day and generation. One cannot but admire the energy and enthusiasm she must have expended on all her multifarious occupations as wife, mother, hostess, writer, printer and bookseller. Her death from asthma in 1778 was deeply regretted by her family and associates. Two obituaries have come down to us. The first is from a friend of her husband's, who said that, in Mrs. Slack, the republic of letters had lost one of its brightest ornaments and that her distinguished character would be revered and held sacred by all the sons and daughters of science. The second appeared in the *Newcastle Chronicle*, presumably with the cognizance of her husband, who survived her by six years. It is tucked away in an inconspicuous corner and completely non-committal, merely stating that

> Her character through life, in her family as well as social connections is so well known as need not be enlarged upon here, and the loss sustained by her death to all her relations and connections will be long and deeply felt.

If we steer a mid-course between the two accounts, one bald, the other fulsome, we shall arrive at a just estimate of the work and influence of Anne Slack.

NOTES

1. 23 February 1708/9.
2. This account is largely based upon a narrative written by herself and found among George Ballard's MSS. in the Bodleian Library, Oxford.

9
SOME FRENCHMEN

In 1792 the French National Assembly decreed that all ecclesiastics who had not taken the civil oath should leave the kingdom within fifteen days and their lands and properties be sold for the benefit of the State. Thousands of Frenchmen, for loyalty to their king, were thus driven into exile, some to Holland, many to England. Four years later, three ships of weary refugees were signalled in Shields harbour. They numbered over three hundred and, owing to great difficulty in housing them, they had to part company and settle in various parts of Northumberland. Some thirty-eight lived in a row of cottages at Heddon Square, known as Frenchman's Row, which were to be their home until the signing of the Peace of Amiens in 1802.

One wonders what they thought of the somewhat premature rejoicings which went on in Newcastle when the peace preliminaries were ratified. News of the ratification was received on 12 October 1801, and the town proceeded to celebrate, on the following Thursday, the end of a war of which the whole country was heartily sick. Church bells rang throughout the day, guns were fired from flag-bedecked ships in the river, while the Newcastle and Gateshead Volunteers fired volleys on the Sandhill and after well-earned refreshment provided by Major Davidson, finished off with a *feu-de-joie* in front of his house in Westgate Street. A moonlit, starry night looked down upon the illuminations and transparencies provided by the Mansion House in the Close, the Fire Office in the Side, the banks in Dean Street and Mosley Street, the saddler in the Bigg Market, and sundry patriotic private citizens in Pilgrim Street and Westgate Street. The exiles had to wait until the following year before they could be repatriated.

Frenchman's Row in the eighteenth century

These exiles had not kept aloof from the everyday life of the people among whom they found shelter and they had been happy in so far as anyone can be happy when driven from ones native land. They were no parasites. It is thought that all such refugees enjoyed an allowance of one shilling a day from the British Government but the Throckley community made themselves into self-supporting citizens. Some acted as tutors and some played their part in the opening of the old St. Andrew's Roman Catholic Church in Newcastle.

When it was safe for them to return to France, they left three of their brethren behind in Heddon churchyard, at rest in the land which gave them asylum. On their departure, the survivors sent a letter expressing their thanks to the Newcastle committee, which had originally received them, and to all those who had shown them kindness during their ten years' stay. With their own hands they made a tangible reminder of their sojourn in the form of a sundial fixed to the wall of one of the cottages. It bore the inscription *Quam signare piis gaudes*,

Frenchman's Row and the Royal French Arms (1957)

gens hospita, donis, prospera sit semper quaelibet hora tibi. 1802. (May each hour which you, hospitable race, delight to mark with affectionate gifts, be always fortunate for you.)

Over a century and a half has passed, bringing wars on a scale that no man then dreamed of, but Frenchman's Row and the sundial, renovated and with a different inscription, *Le Temps passe, le Souvenir reste* (Time passes, Memory remains), are still there, facing a West Road which has changed vastly more than they have, and at one end stands the Royal French Arms with the fleur-de-lis of the Kings of France on its inn-sign.[1]

So the exiles left their abiding mark. What of their bitter opponent, the man whom Sir Walter Scott dubbed a wolf and Thomas Carlyle an obscene spectrum, the self-styled apostle and martyr of liberty, the man whom his fellow-countryman Lamartine stigmatized as the modern Tiberius? What of Jean-Paul Marat? For Marat, too, enjoyed the hospitality of Newcastle twenty years before the men over whose exile he gloated.

What traces of his visit has he left behind?

Marat was a man of many parts. He assimilated foreign languages with ease and his English, if not idiomatic, was fluent. His published work is readable and it is to his credit that he was one of very few Frenchmen of his times who had any command of written English. He had, too, a working knowledge of Italian, Spanish, German and Dutch, which he considered adequate qualification for calling himself a cosmopolitan. He realized that first-hand acquaintance with the countries whose language he studied would strengthen this claim and he seems to have travelled extensively between 1761 and 1775, spending much of his time in England. Whatever he acquired from his travels, it was certainly not poise. He never learned to keep still and his rather hoarse, thin voice was not improved by a pronounced lisp.

In addition to his linguistic studies, Marat also dabbled in medicine, both human and veterinary, and indeed claimed to be a fully qualified doctor, but his claim has yet to be satisfactorily substantiated. His *Philosophical Essay on Man* (1773), which discussed the influence of mind on body and body on mind, had a better reception in England than in France, largely because he allowed his growing political feelings to intrude and annoyed Helvétius by a personal attack. A memoir on the uses of electricity appeared next. Electrotherapy was then in its infancy and, as no one at that time had more than a vague knowledge of the effects of electricity upon human ailments, Marat stood in little danger of contradiction, which he never could brook. According to his own account, he was known in Paris as the 'Doctor of the Incurables,' thanks to the sensational cures he effected where all the accredited practitioners of the Faculty had failed. His success, he said, caused his rivals to calculate with pain the size of his fees and to conspire together for the purpose of defaming him. One of his patients, Monseigneur de Salamon, was less impressed with Marat's ability. He consulted Marat, then veterinary surgeon to the Comte d'Artois, on his own behalf. On taking his prescription to the chemist, the latter exclaimed:

'This medicine is not for you, my lord—it is a horse-mixture!' This was not the only occasion on which the strangeness of Marat's prescriptions alarmed the pharmacist.

Jean-Paul Marat

From medicine Marat turned his attention to a study of heat, light and electricity. With considerable boldness he contradicted Newton's theories and after translating into French Newton's *Optics*, himself wrote a treatise on the same subject which had the effect, in France at least, of encouraging fresh experimental work, most of which was directed towards disproving the validity of Newton's theories. The Académie de Lyon offered a physics prize for the best thesis to determine whether the experiments on which Newton established the different refrangibility of heterogeneous rays were decisive or illusory. Marat competed with alacrity. He was digusted, and expressed his disgust in no uncertain terms, to find that the prize was awarded to a supporter of Newton, while he was merely one of eight who were short-listed. As usual, he thought himself ill-used and slighted and gave vent to an ill-tempered outburst. 'What does Newton matter to me? I prove that his experiments were illusory. I classify five absolutely new phenomena. I add proof so complete that, at the sight of one of these truths, Newton himself would hastily abandon his system.'

Turning once more to the field of electricity, Marat brought himself into prominence again. He conducted at least two hundred experiments, which he set down and discussed with unusual logic and precision. As developments in electricity were progressing rather slowly at that period, Marat's contributions received considerable attention both in France and abroad. Professors from Stockholm and Leipzig went to Paris to watch his experiments and his conclusions were discussed in French and English periodicals. Yet, as on previous occasions, he found that he had his opponents and he resented the fact. His unconcealed pleasure in running counter to all accepted theories, his destructive criticism, his dogmatic boastfulness and petty jealousies, his very originality were not traits likely to endear him to conservative scientists.

They were, however, the traits of the budding political revolutionary and they were the make-up of the man who came to London in 1767 and in 1770 to Newcastle, where he spent three years.

What he had done in France he continued to do, to a varying degree, in England. He made a limited use of his linguistic abilities by teaching French and by writing in English for publication. Among his friends in London, where he lived in the then aristocratic neighbourhood of Soho, was Franklin, the English physicist, with whom he frequently conducted optical experiments. He devoted most of his time, however, to practising medicine and to disseminating revolutionary ideas.

Despite his protestations, Marat was never legally entitled to practice medicine in the British Isles. In 1775, on the occasion of a second visit across the Channel, he had conferred upon him, according to Phipson,[2] the honorary degree of

Doctor of Medicine of St. Andrew's University. The text of the diploma indicated that the honour was bestowed on him in recognition of his great skill in all branches of medicine and the high esteem in which he was held by numerous doctors who approved his work. The actual recommendation for the degree was made by two Edinburgh doctors, Hugh James and William Buchan, and, if one cynical authority is to believed, was obtained on payment of ten guineas. The same authority bluntly states that St. Andrew's was in low water at the time and doubtless glad to collect the fee. The degree thus conferred carried no right to practise either medicine or surgery in England, where a licence was required from the College of Physicians and the Company of Surgeons and this qualification Marat never obtained. He also claimed to hold degrees from Dublin and Edinburgh—a figment of his imagination, but it looked well on his application for the post of veterinary surgeon to the Comte d'Artois, where they duly figured.

To all intents and purposes, Marat was an unqualified practitioner and liable to be branded a quack and impostor. Nevertheless he had his patients and seems to have had considerable success in his new treatment of venereal diseases, upon which he wrote a treatise, *An Essay on Gleets*, in 1775. A reprint was made in England in 1891 by J. B. Bayley, who added that it was well worth reviving, and in 1912 the curious situation arose of a Doctor Payenneville of Rouen, translating the essay into the author's native tongue. Marat claimed to have cured, within months, sufferers who had been unsuccessfully treated for years by the leading doctors of Naples, Rome, Florence, Paris and London. He therefore offered his cure to the London practitioners. The wording of the offer was not such as would give Marat the entrée he sought to that particular circle. He remarked that they seemed to have the monopoly of treating the disease and that people went to them as a matter of custom rather than of faith in their abilities. For the sake of the well-being of society, not to widen the doctors' knowledge, Marat offered his cure. The offer was ignored. A second essay on a disease of the eye, which appeared in the following year, was not presented to the unaccommodating physicians.

There is little doubt that Marat had patients in Newcastle and was well thought of for his work among humans and animals. Tradition said that he was made an honorary Freeman for his services to the town during an epidemic. He may well have been of considerable service in helping to alleviate the distress caused by the disastrous floods of 1771, which affected not only Newcastle but the entire district, and caused great suffering to man and beast, but convincing proof of such service is lacking. No surviving diaries chronicle his visits and there is no record extant of his treatment of animals. Marat, through his frequent visits to Barker and Charnley, the booksellers, must have met Sir Francis Blake Delaval, who foregathered there with Dr. Brown, the vicar of Newcastle, Sir Matthew Ridley, Edward Montagu of Denton Hall, Thomas Bewick, the engraver, Hugh Moises, headmaster of the Royal Grammar School, and all the élite of the town. It would be reasonable to conjecture that Marat's advice might have been sought for the stables at Delaval Hall, but the stable books for the relevant years, 1770–1773, reveal no such link. Certainly Marat was never an honorary Freeman. An exhaustive search into the records, made long ago by Mr. Cail, then Mayor of Newcastle, finally destroyed that legend.

Marat did obtain one elegant parchment from Newcastle. An elaborate document with an imposing seal, it was carefully preserved by Marat's sister, Albertine, and shown by her to Croker of the *Quarterly* on the occasion of his visit to Paris in 1837. The old lady was clearly under the impression that this parchment had conferred on her brother the freedom of Newcastle and Croker failed to examine it carefully. It was, more probably, a document sent to him by one of the patriotic clubs founded in Newcastle in the latter half of the eighteenth century and, according to James Clephan and Joseph Cowen, organized in part, if not entirely, by Marat himself. It was in the nature of an acknowledgement of a presentation copy of Marat's *Chains of Slavery* (1774), in which he set out his

THE

CHAINS OF SLAVERY.

A WORK WHEREIN

THE CLANDESTINE AND VILLAINOUS ATTEMPTS OF

PRINCES TO RUIN LIBERTY

ARE POINTED OUT,

AND THE

DREADFUL SCENES OF DESPOTISM DISCLOSED,

TO WHICH IS PREFIXED,

An ADDRESS to the ELECTORS of GREAT BRITAIN, in order to draw their TIMELY ATTENTION to the Choice of proper REPRESENTATIVES in the next PARLIAMENT.

——*Vitam impendere vero.*

LONDON:

Sold by J. ALMON, oppoſite Burlington Houſe, in Piccadilly; T. PAYNE, at the Mews Gate; and RICHARDSON & URQUHART, near the Royal Exchange.

MDCCLXXIV.

Title Page of 'The Chains of Slavery', in the Library of the Literary and Philosophical Society, Newcastle upon Tyne

political theories at that time.

At the beginning of his stay in England, Marat found himself in a congenial atmosphere where freedom of thought in politics and economics was the order of the day and, by comparison with the repressive censorship across the Channel, there was freedom of speech and of the pen. Marat's first political contact was in London with John Wilkes by whose teaching he was greatly attracted. Wilkes, though a demagogue, was no revolutionary. He attacked, not a limited monarchy, but the absolutism which he accused a Whig oligarchy of exploiting for its own ends. In those early days, Marat followed much the same line of argument. Political discussion and agitation was not confined to the capital. When Marat came to Newcastle, he found he had equal opportunities of airing his views and entering upon debate.

At Barker's and Charnley's, at Sand's circulating library in the Bigg Market, all frequented by Marat, he had the opportunity of listening and contributing to the decorously conducted discussions which took place there. Open for twelve hours a day, they were the regular meeting-place of the prominent citizens of the town, clergy, landed gentry, bankers, school-masters, printers, engravers. More animation and less decorum was shown in the political clubs already mentioned, the Constitutional, the Independent and the Society of Patriots, whose avowed aims were reformatory. The Charter of the Constitutional Club demanded triennial or shorter parliaments, a reduction of the number of placemen and pensioners in the House of Commons, more equal representation of the people and the rescinding of the resolution which gave the seat for Middlesex to Luttrell in place of John Wilkes, whom Marat admired so much. The members of the Independent Club were free burgesses, who met at Sheville's in the Bigg Market and rejected all bribes, gifts or emoluments from any prospective candidates for Parliament and refused to vote for any man, whose electioneering programme did not include the promise to restore the House of Commons to what they termed its 'pristine state'.

Not all the subjects chosen for debate were political. The members had their lighter moments and weighed questions such as whether it would be an advantage in courtship to allow the ladies to make the first advances. The gentlemen came to the conclusion that the question was superfluous as the ladies did so in any case, although their methods were exceedingly discreet and subtle. But the vast majority of the meetings were devoted to discussion upon the pressing political problems of the day. The motion 'Which is the better form of government, a limited monarchy, as in Great Britain, or a republic?' went to the republic by two votes. Yet the clubs seem to have been somewhat inconsistent or undecided in their attitude. One toast list provides some interesting contradictions:

> Our Country and King; the worthy and independent free burgesses of Newcastle; success to the brave Americans in their constitutional resistance; may the storm raised against the Americans burst on the heads of the contrivers; for the restoration of public tranquillity, may their heads be speedily placed on Temple Bar; may the projectors of the famine act perish by famine; may the embers of British liberty be rekindled by American fire.

No wonder Marat thought the time was ripe for launching a revolutionary pamphlet, pamphlet in name but volume in bulk. In 1774, when the town was in a state of excitement over the impending election, Marat published his *Chains of Slavery*, to which he prefixed an address to the electors of Great Britain, to draw their timely attention to the choice of proper representatives in the next parliament. A second edition followed in 1775 and earned a notice in the *Newcastle Chronicle*. It was advertised on sale in Newcastle, Sunderland, Stockton, Durham, Hexham and Alnwick with the comment that it was 'a work well worthy of the attention of the public.' It is interesting to note that the French edition, which Marat brought out in Paris in 1792, does not differ materially in content from the two English editions, so Marat the politician who haunted the local patriotic clubs was in fact the Marat of the Commune.

Marat had decided that the English constitution, which had for long been considered a masterpiece of human wisdom, had become corrupt and, as his ten years in England had allowed him ample opportunity of studying the situation at first hand, he deemed it his duty to expose its vices to his readers. The only sure check on a corrupt government was a parliament of wise and honest men. An election was impending, so this was the time to remind the electorate of their rights and to warn them of the grievous ills that despotism brings in its train. In the address to the electors, Marat attacked, not so much the Crown, as parliamentary corruption.

As long as virtue reigns in the great council of the nations, he said, the prerogatives of the Crown and the rights of the subject are so tempered that they mutually support and restrain each other. But where honour and virtue are wanting in the Senate, the balance is destroyed; Parliament, the strength and glory of Britain, becomes a profligate faction—a band of disguised traitors who, under the name of guardians, traffic away the national interests and the rights of a free-born people: the prince then becomes absolute and the people slaves.

The main work, consisting of sixty-five chapters, was devoted to a detailed attack upon the efforts of princes to subvert liberty. 'The dark projects, crafty proceedings, secret plots, fatal policy and deceitful arts' of royal despots were duly brought to trial and condemned. The essence of the whole pamphlet was that princes can do no right and the people can do no wrong.

Marat assures us that immediately upon publication, his book aroused general enthusiasm and ferment. The reforms he advocated, especially that of more equal representation of the people, became the favourite toast of popular political societies and, thanks to the *Chains of Slavery*, such representation soon became law. The facts are against him, particularly in the hard-headed North. There were in Newcastle, in 1774, thirty-two flourishing incorporated companies. Of these Marat chose the Bricklayers', the Goldsmiths', the Skinners' and Glovers', and the Lumber Troop to be recipients of his work, which he sent by the historic 'Newcastle wagon', so that a large section of the electorate had ample opportunity of imbibing his doctrines before they recorded their votes in one of the most vigorously contested campaigns of the century. There were two opposing parties, the Magistrates', which supported Sir Walter Blackett

Armorial Bearings of the Company of
Skinners and Glovers

and Sir Matthew White Ridley, and the Burgesses', who canvassed for Mr. Thomas Delaval and Captain the Honourable Constantine John Phipps, the Arctic explorer. The incorporated companies had considerable political influence in those days and their votes were eagerly solicited, as freemen of the borough were the sole electors of its Parliamentary representatives. The Skinners' and Glovers' Company was a bad choice on Marat's part, as it was well-known to have aristocratic leanings and numbered among the honorary members six kings, five queens, one prince, nine dukes, two earls and one lord. Among the most active and energetic of the companies, as far as politics were concerned, was the Bricklayers', which admitted Phipps and Delaval to the freedom of their corporation, presenting them with silver trowels and mahogany hods, and voting solidly for them in the election. Of all the companies, only the Bricklayers' and the Joiners' supported the Burgesses' candidates and, despite the bulky ammunition supplied by Marat, Sir Walter Blackett, the 'King of Newcastle' and Sir Matthew White Ridley were returned to Parliament. It is true that enthusiasm was displayed over the 1774 election but it was not fanned by the *Chains of Slavery* and ferment was conspicuously lacking. Murray, in his contemporary account, *The Burgesses' Poll*, states that the election was conducted with the utmost propriety and there was no rowdyism of any sort.

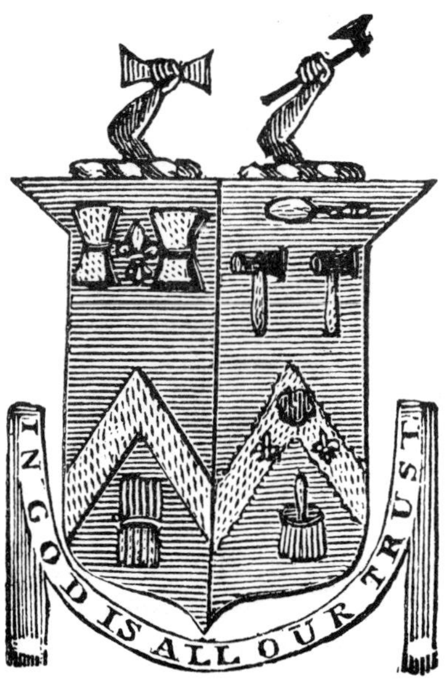

Armorial Bearings of The
Bricklayers' Company

If Marat's imagination ran riot over the influence of the *Chains of Slavery*, it was equally vivid in his account of its composition. While it is admitted that the work is written in vigorous English and shows signs of scholarship and research (a later criticism in the *Newcastle Chronicle* remarked that 'the work is spirited and appears through the whole a masterly execution'), the bald facts are that Marat plodded through thirty weighty tomes of English constitutional history, made extracts and adaptations, welded them together and got the completed volume off to the printers within three months. His own account, inaccurate and highly-coloured, has the merit of being vastly entertaining.

His 'Herculean labour' of 1774 allowed him scarcely two hours sleep a day and the amount of black coffee he drank to keep himself awake nearly killed him. Having despatched the manuscript to the publishers in the confident belief that he had nothing more to do than wait quietly for its success, he fell into a stupor, lasting thirteen days, from which he was roused only by the aid of music and rest. On recovering his faculties, he found that the printer had failed to fulfil his contract. This printer, a Scotsman, was reputed to be in the pay of Lord North, head of the government since 1770, to whom he handed the sheets as they came from the printing press. Incensed at the difficulties put in his way, Marat decided to present almost the whole edition to the patriotic clubs of the North of England, considered, so Marat said, to be the purest in the kingdom. The persecution did not stop there. Lord North set his spies to watch him, bribed his servants, seized his private correspondence and so harried him that for six weeks he slept with his pistols under his pillow, lest North's minions should come and arrest him. Finally, to throw his pursuers off the track, Marat left for Holland and, when he thought all threats to his person were past, returned to the North of England, spending three weeks at Carlisle, Berwick and Newcastle, to visit the clubs which had been the recipients of his book. Everywhere he was fêted, letters of affiliation to three societies were offered to him in a golden casket and the Newcastle clubs levied a subscription and returned to him the entire cost of the publication of the *Chains of Slavery*. Furthermore they financed a second edition, presumably that of 1775, but the Government was still on his track. Emissaries of Lord North stole his beautiful casket and, at the cost of eight thousand guineas, delayed the appearance of his work until after the elections.

The tale is dramatic but it would have been more credible, had some indication of these spectacular happenings been

Westgate Street as Marat saw it

noted in the columns of the local press or in other contemporary records. No such proofs have ever come to light and even Marat's most admiring biographers have been forced to admit that imagination plays a very large part in his narrative.

His visit to Newcastle in 1775 meant that Marat was able to visit yet another new society, founded in that year, and to make the acquaintance of one of its most vociferous and consequently short-lived members, Thomas Spence. A Philosophical Society was established in Westgate Street, with about twenty members, among them Sir Matthew White Ridley, the recent successful candidate for Parliament and Mr. Chapman, the engineer, but the society survived only two or three years. Its purpose, as one of the rules states, was

> to enable its members to speak with facility on every subject that comes before them, to collect and arrange their ideas and not to admit, without examination, the force of any argument, however specious.

The length of the speeches was limited to eight minutes so careful arrangement of ideas was essential for success, and there was certainly a wide variety of subjects. One evening they debated whether charters granted to particular companies, of a free and exclusive trade to particular places, are an advantage or disadvantage to the nation that grants them. The next meeting set out to answer the question, 'What is virtue?' A third tried to solve the problem of the effect that the stopping of all paper currency would have upon this kingdom and upon those nations which did not stop it also. On one occasion they turned to religious matters and enquired why, if God confers salvation freely, faith is necessary to obtain it. Sometimes they descended to mere priggishness as, for example, when they put on the agenda the question, 'Does an exquisite sensibility of mind make for or against the happiness of the possessor?'

Marat cannot have felt at home during some of these discussions and he must have disapproved of at least two of the society's rules. One states that questions might be discussed only with that freedom of debate which is consistent with a decent attention to those established opinions, on the belief in which the welfare of society in a great measure depends. As Marat spent his whole life tilting at established opinions, he cannot have subscribed to this ruling, nor can he have accepted with equanimity their terms of expulsion, incurred by any attempt to injure the society by scandalous aspersions, refusing to comply with the rules or outrageously violating good order and decorum. These prohibitions go a long way towards disproving a rumour that Marat was one of the founders of the Philosophical Society.

So far as we know, Marat behaved with the utmost decorum during his visits. Not so his friend, Thomas Spence, who failed to observe the rules and was ejected. Spence, who had a school in the Broad Chare, was a sincere Liberal, like his acquaintance Thomas Bewick, but of more advanced views. Membership of the society gave him a chance to mix with men of wealth and culture, whose support would have been invaluable to him as a social reformer. Unfortunately he was not content to go slowly and make his position secure. When the society was only eight months old, he sought and received permission to read a paper. He chose one of his favourite topics, 'Property in Land Everyone's Right.' Landlords were to be abolished and all land held by the parishes, which were given wider powers. Every man in the parish was to have a vote, recorded by secret ballot, and to pay his rent into the parish box. The money thus collected was to pay taxes, relieve the poor, pay the salaries of clergymen and schoolmasters, build and repair houses and bridges, make and maintain canals, replant waste land, provide weapons of defence, offer premiums for the encouragement of agriculture. In short, it was to do 'whatever the people thought proper.' The most valuable feature of this interesting and courageous paper was that it showed the widening trend of thought in those times, which had a great effect upon French thinkers and was to develop so rapidly in France into revolution and bloodshed.

No record exists of the reception this thesis received but immediately afterwards Spence had it printed and published. His fellow members were so incensed at his action, which appeared to lend the society's sanction to 'the erroneous and dangerous levelling principles with which the lecture was replete,' that they formally expelled him. Ironically enough, if the society is remembered at all, it is for this paper which it disclaimed with such vigour. Spence eventually left Newcastle for London, where he brought out a penny weekly paper, called *Pig's Meat, or Lessons for the People*, alias (according to Burke), *the Swinish Multitude.* One wonders whether Marat, who did not leave England for some years afterwards, ever had the opportunity of reading it. Its purpose:

> to promote among the labouring part of mankind proper ideas of their situation, of their importance and of their rights, and to convince them that their forlorn condition has not entirely been forgotten and overlooked, nor their just cause unpleaded,

and much of its content would have given him the greatest satisfaction. A plea for freedom of speech—'in those wretched countries where a man cannot call his tongue his own, he can scarce call anything else his own'; the rights of man; government by the people—'laws were made for the governed, not the governor; and all government originates with the people'; equality—'all men, by nature of their humanity, are equal,' venal parliaments—'You were deputed here by the people to get grievances redressed; are not yourselves become the greatest grievance?'; the government of Hell is an absolute monarchy: all these themes occur again and again in Marat's teaching.

Paper XXX contained 'A Song to be sung an Hundred Years Hence' written by Spence to the tune 'Hearts of Oak' Marat would have echoed its sentiments, but they did not become fact for nearly two hundred years. They express the spirit of the days of the Liberation of France in the Second World War and the tyranny they attack was a very different tyranny from that envisaged by Spence and Marat.

Come cheer up my lads; lo! the day draweth near,
When Britain's brave sons freedom's standard will rear;
And joining with Frenchmen, all tyrants o'erthrow,
Th' oppressed releasing wherever they go.

Chorus:

Then mankind rejoice,
France and Britain agree;
Their faiths they have plighted,
Fleets and armies united,
To drive tyrants from you,
And set the world free.

The extract that summarizes Marat himself, his character, his actions and their grievous result is to be found in an essay on the advantages of freedom of speech.

The more men express of their hate and resentment, perhaps the less they retain, and sometimes they vent the whole that way; but these passions, where they are smothered, will be apt to fester, to grow venomous, and to discharge themselves by a more dangerous organism than the mouth; even by an armed and vindicative hand.

So Marat left Newcastle for the last time. When, in 1793, his 'hate and resentment,' his 'armed and vindicative hand' were stilled by Charlotte Corday's knife, not one reference to his assassination appeared in the columns of the local press. This is the more strange as James Losh, Recorder of Newcastle,

The Assassination of Marat, 1793

had visited Paris in 1792, when the *Sans-culotte* despotism, encouraged by Marat and the Commune, was at its height. Some say that Losh, a man of aristocratic bearing, owed his safety in the dangerous streets of Paris to Marat's protection. Whether this is true or not, Losh can scarcely have failed to see Marat during his visit and it is to be regretted that Losh did not think it necessary or desirable to make any comment on Marat's violent end. Losh may well have seen Marat when the latter was in Newcastle. A statement in the *Newcastle Weekly Chronicle* of 25 October 1873, to the effect that the late Mr. Losh frequently mentioned to people then living that, when quite young, he had known Marat as a visitor to his father's house at Woodside, may have some truth in it, although he can scarcely have been out of the nursery. He was born in 1763. Certainly Losh could not have pointed out, as the writer avers, a vacant plot opposite the *Chronicle* Office as the place where Marat and he walked and conversed.

What happened to the copies of Marat's revolutionary pamphlet, the *Chains of Slavery*, which he distributed in Newcastle with such a lavish hand? Almost all have disappeared. In 1878 a blustering March wind blew to the feet of a townsman of Newcastle some greasy papers, which had apparently been used for wrapping butter or bacon. Neither shopkeeper not customer had had any idea of the rarity of the wrapper, which the pedestrian picked up and found to be pages 35–38 of the *Chains of Slavery*. The *Newcastle Chronicle* of 1793 mentions two extant copies. One belonged to the Skinners' and Glovers' Company, 'the obliterating of Time having dimmed the donor's words of dedication until hardly a powerful glass would make them decipherable.' The other found its way into the antiquarian collection of Thomas Bell. Today there are four accessible copies in Newcastle. Thomas Bell's copy is in the library of the Literary and Philosophical Society; another is housed in the Central Reference Library, while the University has one in the Bradshaw collection and one in the White collection, which may well have belonged to James Clephan.

NOTES

1. Frenchman's Row was rebuilt, 1961–62. The character of the row was preserved and a new sundial and gnomon, similar to the original, erected. A bronze plaque commemorates the modernization. Information supplied by F. Austin Child, Chartered Architect.
2. S. L. Phipson, *Jean-Paul Marat*, London, 1924.

10

AS OTHERS SAW US

NOT NEWCASTLE! In Scotland, isn't it? Inaccessible! Cold! Bleak! Nothing but dirty coal-mines. And the people—ignorant, uncouth! Speak some foreign lingo, I believe.

The heart-felt protests of a modern executive directed to work in the North-East? No: the preconceived prejudices of a succession of eighteenth-century visitors, many of whom stayed long enough to modify their views and had reason to be grateful for what Newcastle offered them.

By contrast with the favourite resorts of London society—Bath, Tunbridge Wells, Brighton—Newcastle was indeed remote. Even so, it was sixty miles south of the Border and over a hundred from Edinburgh, reputedly the northern outpost of gentility. Nor was it inaccessible. Stout ships, many of them Tyne-built, plied between the two capitals, calling at Newcastle. It is true that they ran a twofold risk. To the normal hazards of the sea was added the ever-present danger of attack by enemy naval forces or by privateers. As early as 1709 Newcastle Common Council pleaded for two cruisers to protect the Northumbrian coast, only to be told that their ships must sail under escort, but the master of a fast-sailing vessel would deliberately break convoy to forestall the markets while brazenly accusing the naval commanders of poor seamanship. A sea voyage was, therefore, unattractive for most travellers who preferred the lesser perils of dry land.

In those days road surfaces were bad and transport was slow. Dr. Stukeley noted in his diary (December 1748) that a dog was taken from London to Newcastle by ship, fed and turned loose at the same time that a letter was posted to his master in London. The dog had never been in Newcastle before but it arrived home first. Yet the Great North Road was no worse than any other. The most notorious stretch, dreaded by coachmen, lay north of Newcastle, at Gosforth. In 1745 Newcastle Corporation had remade the road from Barras Bridge to the end of the Cow Causey and the Northumberland authorities undertook repairs, evidently inadequate, from that point to Belford for, twenty years later, one of the Edinburgh wagons stuck fast, despite the efforts of nineteen sturdy horses.

As for the footpads and highwaymen who, undeterred by the sight of captured associates dangling from the local gibbet, lay in wait for the unwary, it must be admitted that Gateshead Fell was one of their favourite bases. On the other hand there is no record of a highwayman being chased through the streets of Newcastle, whereas in London, late in the century, a young man halted his stroll down Ludgate Hill agape at the sight of William Hawke, the 'Flying Highwayman', who galloped past, hotly pursued by a yelling mob, and disappeared round a corner leading, ironically enough, to Newgate prison.

None of our visitors were troubled by these gentlemen of the road. John Wesley who, in the course of his long life, covered 100,000 miles of British roads and frequently came to Newcastle never mentions such an encounter. He often rode alone, always unarmed, jogging placidly along with an improving book propped up before him. Less trusting horsemen looked to their pistols and kept within hailing distance of the mailcoach which rumbled into Newcastle, guarded in front by a rider with a drawn sword and behind by another with loaded blunderbuss.

In 1712 you could, for £4. 10s. 0d., go by coach from

London to Edinburgh 'in thirteen days without any stoppage (if God permit)' as the advertisement prudently intimated.[1] No intimation was given that the unsprung vehicle was incredibly uncomfortable. By 1782 steel-sprung stage-coaches left Newcastle daily for the North, South and West and the three-day journey to London cost only £2. 10s. 0d. The wealthy had their own equipages and servants to protect them. Those who put elegance before roadworthiness often came to grief between Grantham and Newark where, after heavy rain, flood-water surged up through the floor-boards of any low-slung vehicle. The higher public coaches had their advantages.

By these various means a stream of celebrities came to Newcastle. Among them were Dr. Johnson and his faithful Boswell, Dr. Gregory of Edinburgh University, Dr. Carlyle of Inveresk, John and Charles Wesley, the Bishops of Ossory and Gloucester, Burns, Defoe, Goldsmith, Smollett, Sterne, the Montagus and William Herschel, then known only as a musician. Sterne, whose arrival was duly chronicled in the local press, maintained that travel is prompted by infirmity of body, imbecility of mind or inevitable necessity, the creator of 'peregrine martyrs'. Most of these notables assigned themselves to the third category.

What did they find on their arrival? Newcastle was then a thriving manufacturing town and port, whose population rose during the century from 18,000 to 28,000 with a corresponding increase in revenue from £8,056, 1s. 1¼d. to £25,699, 0s. 10½d. in 1780 when the Corporation had a gratifying balance of some £2,500. The narrow streets and slum property by the river were no concern of our guests who stayed with friends in elegant houses with large gardens or put up at one of many famous inns. As darkness fell these fashionable neighbourhoods were plunged in gloom. The Corporation lit its seven street lamps[2] on a moonless night but, as they were sited in the less salubrious districts, men of fashion depended upon servants with links or lanthorns to guide them to their dinners, masquerades, concerts, plays, card parties and cockfights. There was entertainment to suit all tastes by night and by day.

Tynemouth Castle and Bathing Place in the Eighteenth Century. From the original by W. Le Petit.

By courtesy of the Librarian, University of Newcastle upon Tyne

There was fishing, shooting and hunting when, at the opening of the season, the Newcastle Hunt met at the White Hart in the Cloth Market with hounds, horns and much cracking of whips. The assizes ushered in a round of races, civic banquets, country-house parties, expeditions to the pretty villages of Wallsend, Elswick or Tynemouth, much favoured for sea-bathing and the drinking of salt water. Contemporary diarists tell us that the weather was generally agreeable. On May Day 1769, Dr. Carlyle found it so hot that he could scarcely walk the two hundred yards between Sir Walter Blackett's summer residence and Wallsend Parish Church.

Towards the end of his life Wesley referred to Newcastle as 'this lovely place' and was reluctant to part from its 'lovely people'. Over the years he had learnt to appreciate the canny Novocastrian who, on first acquaintance, concealed his innate warmth and generosity under a cloak of blunt independence.

The educated townsfolk were neither ignorant nor uncouth. They kept abreast of the latest fashions in dress and social graces. They were certainly keen business men, alive to the problems of export and import, profit and loss, but in their leisure moments they frequented coffee-houses and circulating libraries which were in effect literary coteries where books, art, philosophy and politics were discussed by such diverse habitués as the Vicar, Sir Matthew Ridley, Sir Francis Delaval, Thomas Bewick, Dr. Moises, Master of the Grammar School, and Aubone Surtees, the banker. They were no strangers to the King's English, but the humbler inhabitants were difficult to understand.[3] Theirs was a dialect inherited from bygone invaders, Scots, Norsemen, Angles, woven down the ages into a colourful vernacular, which found no place in Dr. Johnson's famous dictionary. Such words as *crankie*, *black endies*, *marra*, *gowk*, *hinny*, were either beneath or beyond his ken. As for the all-embracing *canny*, applicable in a flattering sense to places and people alike, that had to wait yet another century for official recognition[4] and even then it was given the restricted Scottish meaning of cautious or frugal.

Strange-sounding words were further complicated by the local burr which gave Newcastle the nickname of Burcastle, capital of Croakumshire. The subtle differences in the *r* as pronounced by the Lowland Scots, Northumbrians, Novocastrians and the folk of Shields, completely eluded the ear of critical visitors who dubbed them all a disagreeable provincialism. Tynesiders were—and are—intensely proud of their 'manly Doric' which some claimed to have inherited from Harry Hotspur, others from Saint Cuthbert. Richard Dawes, at one time Master of the Grammar School but not himself a Novocastrian, wrote, tongue in cheek, a poem wherein he suggested that the burr was a punishment inflicted by the Devil upon the citizens, 'a rude, unpolish'd, cut-throat Band' and therefore his peculiar property, who had shown unwelcome signs of becoming civilized. To all harsh critics the unruffled Geordie slyly pointed out that the honourable members had no difficulty in understanding Lord Eldon, son of a Newcastle hostman, when he rose to p*r*o*r*ogue parliament.

As the author of *The Newcastle Rider* says:

> Men's minds and likewise their opinions
> Are various as the size of onions.

Daniel Defoe *c.* 1706

By courtesy of the Librarian, University of Newcastle upon Tyne

Such dissimilarity is indeed apparent in three of our eighteenth-century visitors, Daniel Defoe, Oliver Goldsmith and Mrs. Elizabeth Montagu.

One night in late September 1706, Defoe, armed to the teeth and leading a spare horse, clattered over Tyne Bridge to rendezvous with John Bell, the postmaster. Defoe had then embarked upon the second stage of his career; he was a government agent, employed by Robert Harley, Earl of Oxford, to sound the reactions of the North towards the proposed union of England and Scotland and 'in conversation and by all Reasonable Methods to Dispose people's minds to the Union.'

He travelled incognito as Alexander Goldsmith but Bell knew who he was. Bell was himself an agent, in contact with Fearns, another secret serviceman, sent to Edinburgh by Harley to keep a sharp eye on Defoe. Bell was paid £50 a year for his official work, and like most provincial postmasters, was encouraged to keep an inn with the monopoly of providing mounts for all travellers riding post. He was, therefore, in an unrivalled position for overhearing and reporting to London everything of moment that occurred in his neighbourhood. Moreover the postmaster could, and did exercise a long-established practice[5] of opening, detaining or copying letters, with or without warrant. The more delicate the political situation, the more useful to the government was the country postmaster.

Defoe, well aware of the system, was too prudent to divulge any secrets to Bell as they chatted over their wine, awaiting a fresh horse for one of Defoe's had gone lame after what he described as a severe journey. He was also short of cash. He never carried much money and in 1697, had advocated the transference of funds by book-entries, listing Newcastle as a suitable centre, to obviate the risk of dispatching by road large sums which might end up in a highwayman's pocket. Defoe did rather well out of mine host who had to apply to Harley for the reimbursement of £60. 17s. 6d.: item, one horse, £15. 17s. 6d.; item, cash £25; item, letter of credit, £20. Bell clearly had misgivings about the suitability of a writer for under-cover work but he told Harley that Defoe appeared capable and wished him every success in his mission.

Defoe did not return the compliment. Before his visit in 1710, this time under the name of Claude Guilot, the union of England and Scotland had been achieved. He was now sent, again by Harley, to ferret out the relative strength of Whigs,

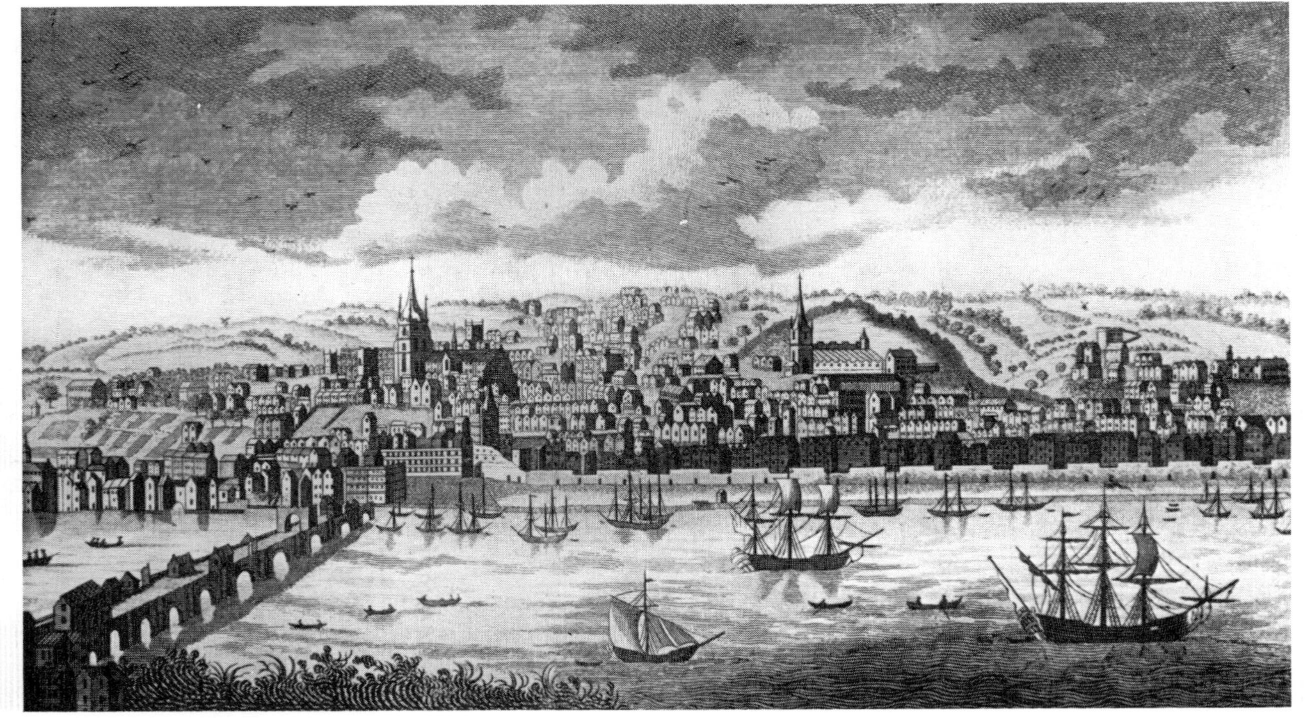

Eighteenth Century Newcastle upon Tyne from Hillgate Street. As described by Defoe in 'A Tour through England and Wales'

By courtesy of the Director and Curator, Laing Art Gallery, Newcastle upon Tyne

Tories and Jacobites. Bell, mistakenly believing that Defoe was Godolphin's emissary and therefore pro-Whig, spread rumours to that effect throughout the town. Defoe shrewdly extracted travelling expenses from the postmaster and proceeded to advise Harley that Bell was no longer to be trusted, that he would never again use this source of supplies, however straitened his circumstances, and that any hope of a satisfactory conclusion to his mission must be abandoned.

Righteous indignation did not prevent Defoe from spending much of the next two years in the district. Mindful perhaps of the old saying—'You must go to Gateshead to hear Newcastle news'—he found lodgings in Hillgate Street, whence he had an uninterrupted view of 'a noble, large and deep river, a strong and stately stone bridge, the longest and largest quay for landing and lading goods that is to be seen in England' and a dreary town on the landward side.[6]

At this period he exploited Joseph Button, a bookseller on the bridge, who published the original *Newcastle Gazette* in which Defoe is reputed to have collaborated. Button's work was cheap but inaccurate, as he cheerfully admitted in his sole surviving letter to Defoe who, attracted by the low price, entrusted Button with the first edition of his *British Visions*, a kind of Old Moore's Almanac with political connotations, and *The Family Instructor*, a series of improving dialogues on Christian behaviour. Nor did he hesitate to use his publisher as an errand-boy, detailed to see to the repair of his spectacles, the supply of his favourite pickles or the lodging of his protégés whom Mrs. Button, weary of looking after a houseful of apprentices, refused to accept. Button's good offices were ill-rewarded. In the later London edition of *The Family Instructor* Defoe allowed outspoken censure of Button's cheaper production to appear in the preface.

It was long maintained that Defoe wrote *Robinson Crusoe* in Gateshead. The tradition was fostered by the existence of a local tavern of that name with an appropriate sign, painted by Collier. Hilton, the Gateshead-born poet, proudly wrote (1774):

> if strong report say true,
> 'Twas in this place the bold design he drew.
> GATESHEAD, scarce known, the hardy Writer chose;
> When sorely prest by persecuting foes.

Alas for civic pride! The immortal classic was penned at Stoke Newington. Defoe, indifferent to persecuting foes, was at the time heavily involved in Tyneside labour troubles.

Although he had little patience with the 'Shibboleth upon their tongues' and still less with their claim that it proved the antiquity of their origin, although, as an employer, he always aimed at the maximum output for the minimum outlay, Defoe showed practical sympathy for all workers in the coal trade, especially the keelmen. Was he actuated by a compulsive antipathy towards the gentry and successful merchants? Was he by nature a trouble-maker encouraging, as Henry Riddell, owner of the Coachy Field pit at Ravensworth, complained in 1711, 'a refractoriness among that sort of people'? Was he seeking some personal advantage as his enemies insinuated or was he an unbiased champion of the underdog?

Coal-owners, miners, hostmen, collier masters and keelmen were interdependent but their conflicting interests continually fomented disputes.

At the beginning of the century when export figures showed a substantial annual increase, the owners faced the problem of expansion, downwards or laterally, but they lacked the technical skills necessary for the former and the cost of renting way-leaves for the latter[7] and maintaining the timbered wagonways was enormous. Rising costs meant rising retail prices and, invariably, sharp repercussions from the London market. In a working day pitmen could earn twice as much as other labourers but were frequently laid off when coal was stock-piled because of bad weather, enemy action or a keelmen's strike which kept the colliers in port, with the result that their average wage was low. Colliers were paid—sometimes as little as £2. 10s. 0d. if the market was poor—for the round trip from Newcastle to London which took four to six weeks. The masters expected danger money for a run like that of December 1711, when twenty-five colliers were driven inshore by three French men-of-war and three privateers. If their sailing date was delayed because they had been forced to await a naval escort, they claimed compensation for lost time. As some six hundred colliers were in service, large sums were involved and the cost passed on to the consumer. Defoe urged that an insurance scheme be evolved to keep prices steady but his proposal was turned down.

The king-pins of the trade were the keelmen, who ferried the coal from the staithes up-river to the colliers berthed in the harbour. When they went on strike pits and colliers lay idle. About 1,500 strong and a closely-knit community, they lived in Sandgate, the Wapping of Newcastle. They were tough men, doing a tough job in which they were particularly vulnerable to attack from press-gangs who ambushed the three-men crews as they came ashore. In 1705 Defoe had prepared a report for the Select Committee of the House of Lords, calling for the abolition of impressment and offering alternative methods of recruitment for the Royal Navy. Again he was defeated[8] but undaunted.

His hour of triumph came in 1712. In his politico-economic *Review* he once more championed the keelmen's cause. By a voluntary levy of 4d. a tide they had amassed £2,000 and built a hospital for their sick and needy. After nine years of maladministration they went on strike and demanded representation on the governing body. They further petitioned the Crown for a charter to give them direct control. This step was opposed by the outraged magistrates and hostmen who wanted to run the hospital themselves and keep a tight hold on the men. Defoe's vigorous article in the *Review* swayed London opinion. The Commons decided in favour of the keelmen who long continued to be a thorn in the flesh to the disgruntled hostmen.

Unlike Defoe, Goldsmith was anxious to get out of Newcastle as quickly as possible. His anxiety is understandable. All he saw of the town was the inside of a tavern and of Newgate

The Keelmen's Hospital

By courtesy of the Director and Curator, Laing Art Gallery, Newcastle upon Tyne

gaol—if what he told his Uncle Contarine was true.

Having obtained his B.A. at Dublin, Goldsmith had toyed with and discarded the idea of studying law, felt a sudden enthusiasm for a medical career and in 1752, appeared in Edinburgh, ostensibly to read medicine. His assets were a modest sum contributed by his uncle, who never lost faith in him, and an unquenchable, though generally groundless, optimism. On the debit side stood his inability to concentrate on any syllabus, complete indifference to public opinion, carelessness over money matters and a longing to be of consequence which led him to make strange acquaintances and to distort the truth with astounding exaggerations.

Goldsmith neglected the lecture-room for the livelier society of so-called friends whose debts he gaily shouldered when he had no means of paying his own. It took him the greater part of 1753 to settle a bill for sky-blue satin and shalloon, black Genoa velvet and other fashionable materials, whereupon he

Oliver Goldsmith, painted by Sir Joshua Reynolds
By courtesy of the Librarian, University of Newcastle upon Tyne

promptly opened an even larger account which was still outstanding when he decided he could further his studies more profitably under distinguished professors at the Sorbonne and Leyden.

A letter to Uncle Contarine, written at Leyden in May 1754, gives us Goldsmith's account of what transpired. At the beginning of the year he had gone to Leith where a Scottish ship, the *Saint Andrew*, master John Watt, was about to sail for Bordeaux. The boat looked seaworthy and he was assured of six agreeable companions on the voyage. Goldsmith sailed with her. Two days later, she ran into heavy weather and had to make for shelter in the Tyne. The passengers went ashore but got no further than an inn where they spent the evening carousing. In the midst of the merry-making the door burst open, in marched a sergeant and twelve grenadiers with fixed bayonets, who arrested the revellers and escorted them to Newgate on the charge of being French agents working for the Jacobite cause—a charge of which Goldsmith was innocent. At that time he had no strong political leanings.

Goldsmith's reactions to this untoward situation were typical. He was unperturbed where other men would have voiced angry protests against wrongful detention. He saw in it the hand of providence for he later heard that the *Saint Andrew* foundered in the Bay of Biscay with the loss of all hands. Thankful to be alive, he was disproportionately upset because his luggage went down with the ship. His main concern was that the university authorities might learn of his dilemma and withhold a degree—an irrelevant point as he had already left without completing the course. Nevertheless Goldsmith begged his uncle to keep the affair secret or to say he had been imprisoned for debt.

Here Goldsmith's story becomes confused. An unauthenticated tradition says that he was never in Newcastle but found lodgings in Sunderland where he was arrested for the unpaid debt incurred in Edinburgh. From this predicament he was rescued by two fellow-students, Dr. Sleigh and Lauchlan Macleane, later under-secretary in the Grafton ministry. Goldsmith himself infers that these gentlemen procured his release from Newgate, that he went to Sunderland to seek passage on another ship and was there tracked down by the bailiffs. Was he trying to hoodwink his friends or his uncle? Was he throughout drawing upon his fertile imagination?

It is impossible to substantiate beyond all shadow of doubt his claim to have been a prisoner in Newgate. There are no prison records extant for 1754; no French spy scare was reported in the local press; no *Saint Andrew* appears in the Shields shipping lists. Lloyd's Records go back to 1741 but none were kept for 1754, therefore no recorded movements of vessels exist for that year.[9] One faint surviving clue supports Goldsmith's assertations. In a General letter book Customs 84/323 the following is filed:[10]

To J. Clerland, Esq.
I have enclosed the Surveyors Certificates and Masters Affidavit to secure a Mediterranean Pass for the *Saint Andrew* of Aberdeen, Alexander Goodfellow. Your fee I have received.

Messrs. Robt. and George Udnys will call at the Admiralty Office for the Pass.

I am,
Your most humble servant,
L.S.

1st December 1753.

Except for the master's name everything tallies—the ship's name and nationality, the probable sailing date and final destination.

In his biography of Goldsmith, Washington Irving wrote: 'Scarcely an adventure or character is given in his works that may not be traced to his own parti-coloured story.' Is it over-fanciful to think that the prison scenes in *The History of the Man in Black* and *The Vicar of Wakefield* are based on Goldsmith's personal experiences in Newgate gaol?

The towers of the New Gate had been used as a prison for four centuries. From the battery at the top, where debtors were allowed to exercise, there was an uninterrupted view along Gallowgate and of the gruesome preliminaries when the sheriff waited for the condemned man to be seated on the coffin in a cart drawn up at the gateway. Yet Newgate, throughout the eighteenth century, compared very favourably with its London counterpart.[11]

The Corporation's attitude towards prisoners was consistently enlightened. The garnish, gambling, drinking and brawls, the poor fare, the shackling of felons at the keeper's discretion, the herding together of debtors, first offenders and hardened criminals, the threat of gaol-fever were unchecked but conditions were luxurious compared with those in the dirty, damp guard-chamber of the castle where the accused were chained to staples during their trial and exhibited to sightseers on Assize Sunday at sixpence a head. Except for the condemned cell, the prisoners' quarters were upstairs, airy

Newgate from the North

By courtesy of the Director and Curator, Laing Art Gallery, Newcastle upon Tyne

and clean, with brooms and mops to keep them so. There was an adequate supply of firing and candles, while each occupant had a chaff bed, two blankets and a coverlet, items of which few British prisons could boast. From 1700 the Newcastle authorities had seen to the provision of coal and water, regulated the fees which discharged prisoners had to pay before their final release, obtained the services of a doctor and chaplain. The latter was usually the curate of Saint Andrew's who read prayers twice weekly, preached a monthly sermon, visited any inmate by request and accompanied those under sentence of death to the gallows. Of the medical officers, Dr. Rotherham won public commendation from John Howard in his *State of the Prisons*, as being one of the few throughout the kingdom to attend regularly without payment.

On the whole the Corporation chose their gaolers wisely and treated them with understanding. Normally a gaoler was heavily fined if a prisoner escaped, and Michael Dawson faced a penalty of £40. 3s. 11d. when, in 1747, a smuggler broke out owing to what the Common Council delicately referred to as the 'insufficiency' of the building. The mayor therefore exonerated Dawson, rescinded the fine and hastily sent for a repair gang whose work did not prevent four prisoners from making a successful bid for freedom a few weeks before Goldsmith's arrival. In his report Howard had a special word of praise for the humanity of Newgate gaolers.

The Corporation could, to a great extent, control conditions in the town gaol but not the cause of imprisonment or the sentences imposed in an age when 'numerous penal laws grind every rank of people, and chiefly those least able to resist oppression, the poor.'[12] In Newgate Goldsmith rubbed shoulders with returned transportees, sheep-stealers, abductors, murderers, all condemned to death, petty thieves and faws sentenced to seven years' transportation, and debtors, forced to remain there until they had paid in full. Whichever the charge preferred against him, Goldsmith was fortunate in having influential friends to secure his early release.

An unbroken silence may well be the severest form of censure. Never again did Goldsmith mention Newcastle.

That indefatigable letter-writer and conversationalist, Elizabeth Montagu, joined Sterne's 'peregrine martyrs' in 1758 when she travelled to Newcastle with her husband who had long been guardian of his bed-ridden cousin, John Rogers, now deceased. He was chief heir to Rogers' estates, comprising collieries and farms in South-East Northumberland and Durham, together with a country house, Denton Hall. Edward Montagu accepted with his habitual composure the heavy responsibilities which thus devolved upon him whereas his wife, bewailed the circumstances which made her 'the most busy, miserable woman in the world.'

She had the profound sympathy of her circle. Miss Carter, a fellow blue-stocking, was under the impression that Newcastle lay inside the Arctic Circle and shuddered at the thought of the journey—as did Mrs. Montagu, who was to spend thirty years' travelling between Tyneside and her favourite establishments in London and Berkshire. Yet she never met

Mrs. Elizabeth Montagu by Sir Joshua Reynolds
By courtesy of the City Librarian, Central Reference Library, Newcastle upon Tyne

with any worse mishap than a damp crossing of the flooded Trent in 1765. She never glimpsed a highwayman. Had she done so, she would certainly have reported the encounter with a wealth of detail. On her first visit she brought a stock of provisions to support life in this barren outpost. Two years later, she promised her father some plump game from Northumberland and in 1794, reminded her Scotswood agent to send to Sandleford her usual supply of coal, potatoes, barley, butter, dried salmon and homespun huckaback.

Dr. Monsey, her London physician and admirer, fearing for the health of his hothouse plant, gave her explicit instructions for countering the ailments to which she would undoubtedly be exposed and commended her to Dr. Ramsay's care. Mrs. Montagu, convinced that she could never be happy in Newcastle,[13] noted his advice. Their anxiety was baseless. She withstood the bracing climate uncommonly well; only on two occasions did she summon a doctor and patronized, not Dr. Ramsey, but the more fashionable Dr. Askew.

Lord Lyttleton was also deeply attached to Mrs. Montagu and had disturbing visions of the lady incarcerated at the bottom of a coal-mine. Being a classical scholar and of a poetical turn of mind, he likened her to Proserpinà carried off by Pluto to be queen of Hell, whose inhabitants would express wonder and admiration at her appearance. It is doubtful whether Mrs. Montagu ventured within a hundred yards of a pit-head and there is no record of the miners' reactions to her presence but she had much to say about them.

A commoner herself, Elizabeth Montagu dearly loved a title and never forgot that her husband was a grandson of the Earl of Sandwich, a distinction which the unassuming Edward seems never to have remembered. Throughout her correspondence she pens with obvious delight the names of the élite of the neighbourhood with whom, as chatelaine of the newly-restored Denton Hall and a town house in Pilgrim Street, she exchanged hospitality—the Duke and Duchess of Northumberland, Lord Ravensworth, Sir Walter Blackett, Sir Thomas Clavering of Axwell Park who claimed descent from Charlemagne. The Ords of Fenham, the Bowes of Gibside, families of impeccable ancestry, and the 'principal persons' of the Corporation were also welcome. Mrs. Montagu led a very gay social life. In September 1760, she wrote to Lord Lyttleton:

> I am actually an inhabitant of Newcastle, and am taking out my freedom, not out of a gold box, but by entering into all the diversions of the place. I was at a musical entertainment this morning; I have bespoken a play for tomorrow night, and shall go to a ball, on choosing a mayor, on Monday night.

The events to which she referred were a concert at Springwell Gardens, modelled on Vauxhall and Ranelagh, a performance by the Edinburgh Comedians and the festivities which followed the mayoral banquet in honour of Henry Partis, elected for a second term of office. To Miss Carter she remarked that love of pleasure and dissipation raged here as much, if not as elegantly, as in London. Serious efforts were being made locally to improve the standard of music and the attitude of the audience but one gathers from various sources, including Mrs. Montagu, that people still went to see and be seen rather than to listen and be instructed.

'Montagu speaks and she subdues the world,' said the devoted Dr. Monsey. Her husband's business friends, who clearly had little inclination for the gallantries of a blue-stocking's salon, were deaf to her eloquence and she complained[14] bitterly that

> the conversation always turns upon money; the moment you name a man, you are told what he is worth; the losses he has had, or the profit he has made by coal-mines . . . My mind is not naturally set to this tune.

A strange protest from one who, in her widowhood, assumed control of vast estates, selected agents with unerring judgement, boasted of her Tyneside collieries, farms, bricks, tile and tar factories, of the £36,000 she paid for the property adjoining Denton and of her immense bank balance accumulating in Threadneedle Street. Her nephew and heir, Edward Montagu, who had long been manager of the lucrative Montagu Main pit, benefited by about £10,000 a year.

It is unfortunate that no one chronicled the verbal clashes between Elizabeth Montagu and Dr. Carlyle. They would have made lively reading. The latter, notoriously a lady's man, was far from cordial to the mistress of Denton Hall. In his autobiography he noted accurately, if unflatteringly, that

> in Newcastle . . . her natural character was displayed, which was that of an active manager of her affairs and a keen pursuer of her interest, not to be outdone by the sharpest coal-dealer on Tyne; but in this capacity she was not acting a part.

In her dealings with the pitmen Mrs. Montagu played the

Denton Hall from the Sketch by S. H. Grimm
By courtesy of Northumberland County Archivist

Lady Bountiful but after twenty years' contact with them, failed to penetrate their uncompromising exterior. A letter (1775) to her sister-in-law is illuminating. She described Denton as an anthill swarming with black creatures no better than savages, whose dialect was 'dreadful to the auditor's nerves'. She strongly disapproved of the miners' large families begotten, in her view, for the sole purpose of increasing their 'riches'. Were they not paid more than other labourers? Did not their sons, employed underground from the age of seven, earn as much as a shilling a day? And what did they do with all this money? Spent it on meat and drink, went about in rags and pleaded misery, poverty and oppression.

With scant hope of civilizing the boys before they went into the pits, Mrs. Montagu established a school where the girls were taught to spin, knit and sew. Occasionally she distributed clothing or gave the young folk a dinner but her motives were far from disinterested. She congratulated herself on the small

GATSHEAD

Black-Fryer Gate	L	Pandon-Gate	Y	White-Fryers	9
Morden-Tower	M	Carpenters-Tower	Z	Newgate-Street	10
Ever-Tower	N	Wall Koll & Habkin-Tower		St Andrews-Church	11
Andrew-Tower	O	Sandgate	&c	High Fryer Chare	12
Newgate	P	Ratten-Rawe	1	Darn Crook	13
Bertram-Mumboucher-Tower	Q	Fennel-Street	2	Hucksters Booths	14
Ficket Tower	R	St Johns Church	3	Back Gate of the Black-Fryers	15
Pilgrim-Street-Gate	S	An Alms-House	4		
Carliol-Tower	T	Westmerland-Place	5	White-Cross	16
Plummer-Tower	V	Back-Rawe	6	Fryer-Chare	17
St Austin Tower	W	Touthill	7	Nunn's-Gate	18
Corner-Tower	X	Bailiff-Gate	8	The Earls-Inn	19

outlay involved in providing cheap rice, skimmed milk and coarse beef and on creating a harmonious relationship with her employees who would in gratitude redouble their efforts. Her summing up is a masterpiece of complacency. 'The general coal trade, and my concerns in it are, at present, in a thriving way.'

Most of our visitors were birds of passage whose criticism or condescension neither impressed nor disheartened the inhabitants. Some there were who stayed on, became Tynesiders by adoption and even mastered the local dialect. Let one of them have the last word:

> Bout Lunnen then Div'nt ye mak sic a rout,
> There's nouse there ma winkers to dazzle;
> For a' the fine things ye are gobbin about,
> We can marra iv canny Newcassel.[15]

NOTES

1. *Newcastle Courant*, October 1712.
2. An Act of Parliament (1763) provided for improved lighting to be financed by a rate (max. 6d. in the £) levied on all property owners within the walls. The penalty for vandalism was £10 per lamp or up to three months' hard labour.
3. London criticisms of the 1967 L.P. record, *Waters of Tyne*, indicate that they still are.
4. In Dr. Ogilvie's *Imperial Dictionary*, 1848.
5. The Post Office Act (1711) legalized this practice under warrant.
6. Daniel Defoe: *Tour Through England and Wales* (1724–26).
7. In 1719, the rents varied from £100 to £1,000 per annum.
8. Press-gangs were still active on Tyneside in 1798.
9. Information kindly supplied by Mr. R. C. E. Lander, Shipping Editor of Lloyd's, London
10. Information by courtesy of Mr. E. A. Carson, Librarian and Archivist, H.M. Customs and Excise, King's Beam House, London.
11. *The Universal Magazine*, September 1764.
12. Oliver Goldsmith; *The Citizen of the World*, Letter LXXX (1760).
13. 'Happiness is a flower too delicate to bloom in the latitude of Newcastle.' Mrs. Montagu in a letter to Miss Anne Pitt.
14. In a letter (20/10/58) to Dr. Stillingfleet.
15. *Canny Newcassel*. (T. Thompson). "Then for London don't raise such a shout,/There's naught there my vision to dazzle;/For all the fine things you are bragging about,/We can equal in friendly Newcastle.'